In Re Gault:

DO MINORS HAVE THE SAME RIGHTS AS ADULTS?

SUPREME COURT MILESTONES

In Re Gault:

DO MINORS HAVE THE SAME RIGHTS AS ADULTS?

SUSAN DUDLEY GOLD

Marshall Cavendish
Benchmark
New York

Dedicated to Gertrude Gualtieri Harris, whose dedication as a special education teacher and child advocate has made a difference in the lives of many.

With special thanks to Professor David M. O'Brien of the Woodrow Wilson Department of Politics at the University of Virginia for reviewing the text of this book.

Marshall Cavendish Benchmark
99 White Plains Road
Tarrytown, NY 10591
www.marshallcavendish.us

Library of Congress Cataloging-in-Publication Data

Gold, Susan Dudley.
 In Re Gault : do minors have the same rights as adults? / Susan Dudley Gold.
    p. cm.—(Supreme Court milestones)
 Includes bibliographical references and index.
 ISBN 978-0-7614-2584-7
1. Gault, Gerald Francis, 1949 or 50—Trials, litigation, etc.—Juvenile literature. 2. Juvenile justice, Administration of—United States—Juvenile literature. 3. Due process of law—United States—Juvenile literature. 4. Children—Legal status, laws, etc.—United States—Juvenile literature. 5. Gault, Gerald Francis, 1949 or 50—Trials, litigation, etc. 6. Justice, Administration of. 7. Children's rights. 8. Due process of law. I. Title.

 KF228.G377G655 2007
 345.73'08—dc22

                              2006026392
Photo research by Connie Gardner

Cover Photo: Pixtail/SuperStock

The photographs in this book are used by permission and through the courtesy of:
SuperStock: Pixtail, 2-3; *AP Photo*: 12,48,95,121; Ron Edmonds, 40; *The Granger Collection*: 18,27; *Frank Lewis*: 32; *Norman Dorsen*: 42; *Frank Parks*: 59; *Corbis*: Bettmann, 65,106,108; CORBIS: 116; *Getty*: Bob Gomel/Time Life Pictures, 87.

Publisher: Michelle Bisson
Art Director: Anahid Hamparian
Series Designer: Sonia Chaghatzbanian
Printed in China
1 3 5 6 4 2

contents

THE U.S. BILL OF RIGHTS

As part of an effort to convince the citizens and the states to support the new Constitution, Congress added ten amendments to the original document on September 25, 1789. These first ten amendments to the Constitution became the Bill of Rights. Ratified by the states on December 15, 1791, these ten amendments serve as the centerpiece of individual American liberties. For 176 years, however, until the U.S. Supreme Court ruled in the *In Re Gault* case in 1967, the Bill of Rights did not apply to the juvenile justice system.

AMENDMENT I

Congress shall make no law respecting an establishment of religion, or prohibiting the free exercise thereof; or abridging the freedom of speech, or of the press; or the right of the people peaceably to assemble, and to petition the Government for a redress of grievances.

AMENDMENT II

A well regulated Militia, being necessary to the security of a free State, the right of the people to keep and bear Arms, shall not be infringed.

AMENDMENT III

No Soldier shall, in time of peace be quartered in any house, without the consent of the Owner, nor in time of war, but in a manner to be prescribed by law.

AMENDMENT IV

The right of the people to be secure in their persons, houses, papers, and effects, against unreasonable searches and seizures, shall not be violated, and no Warrants shall issue, but upon probable cause, supported by Oath or affirmation, and particularly describing the place to be searched, and the persons or things to be seized.

AMENDMENT V

No person shall be held to answer for a capital, or otherwise infamous crime, unless on a presentment or indictment of a Grand Jury, except in cases arising in the land or naval forces, or in the Militia, when in actual service in time of War or public danger; nor shall any person be subject for the same offence to be twice put in jeopardy of life or limb; nor shall be compelled in any criminal case to be a witness against himself, nor be deprived of life, liberty, or property, without due process of law; nor shall private property be taken for public use without just compensation.

AMENDMENT VI

In all criminal prosecutions, the accused shall enjoy the right to a speedy and public trial, by an impartial jury of the State and district wherein the crime shall have been committed; which district shall have been previously ascertained by law, and to be informed of the nature and cause of the accusation; to be confronted with the witnesses against him; to have compulsory process for obtaining witnesses in his favor, and to have the assistance of counsel for his defence.

AMENDMENT VII

In Suits at common law, where the value in controversy shall exceed twenty dollars, the right of trial by jury shall be preserved, and no fact tried by a jury shall be otherwise re-examined in any Court of the United States, than according to the rules of the common law.

AMENDMENT VIII

Excessive bail shall not be required, nor excessive fines imposed, nor cruel and unusual punishments inflicted.

AMENDMENT IX

The enumeration in the Constitution of certain rights shall not be construed to deny or disparage others retained by the people.

AMENDMENT X

The powers not delegated to the United States by the Constitution, nor prohibited by it to the States, are reserved to the States respectively, or to the people.

introduction
Rights for Children

WHEN A NEIGHBOR accused fifteen-year-old Gerald Gault of making obscene phone calls, the Arizona youth never dreamed the charge would lead to a six-year sentence in a juvenile detention center. The punishment for an adult convicted of making the same calls would have been a $50 fine or, at the most, two months in jail. But because Gerald was a minor—not yet eighteen years old—the laws of the time required that his case be handled in juvenile court, where a judge had the authority to decide his fate. No lawyer represented Gerald at the hearing on the charges against him. The neighbor never appeared in court and never testified against him. The proceedings were not recorded and were closed to the press. After a brief hearing, the judge in Gerald's case found Gerald guilty of "immoral" behavior and ruled that he would have to stay in a detention center until he turned twenty-one.

The sentence was so outrageous that Gerald's parents, with help from a local attorney, appealed the case to superior court. The case eventually made its way to the U.S. Supreme Court.

On May 15, 1967, the Court ruled for the first time that the Constitution protected the rights of children involved in the criminal justice system. The ruling guaranteed children many of the same rights held by adults: the right to an attorney, the right not to incriminate themselves, the right to face their accusers and to cross-examine them, and the right to be notified of the charges against them. In the 8 to 1 decision, the justices withheld from children only two rights guaranteed adults charged with crimes: the right to a trial by jury and the right to an open hearing. These two exceptions should be maintained, the Court reasoned, to protect the children from publicity. Proceedings involving children should be kept confidential, according to the ruling.

In just this one case—*In re Gault*—juveniles won the guarantee of four separate rights. Adults had won similar guarantees from the U.S. Supreme Court only after arguing—and winning—separate cases for each right.

"The Gault case was tremendously important," said Anthony A. Guarna, longtime chief juvenile probation officer in Pennsylvania's Montgomery County. The case, he said, "solidified the constitutional rights of juveniles" during court procedures.

In reality, however, the Gault decision presented two opposite viewpoints: that juvenile courts were necessary because they helped youthful offenders change their bad behavior (unlike criminal courts that focused on punishment); but that juveniles had to be protected from the juvenile court system (by granting them the four rights).

In the years that followed the decision, states struggled to rework the juvenile justice system to conform to the Gault requirements. The juvenile court today is a mix of the old informality and the new procedures set in place since Gault. Many more young people accused of crimes have lawyers representing them.

Still, in many cases, the juvenile justice system has failed to live up to the promise of the Gault decision. While states endorse the right to counsel, many youngsters waive their right to an attorney before ever consulting a lawyer about their rights. The system lacks resources and personnel, and in many cases treatment programs and institutions do not provide the services youths need.

Some experts believe the Gault ruling helped dismantle the juvenile court and led to the push toward criminal courts for offenders of all ages. A growing number of states have passed laws requiring children accused of violent crimes to be tried in adult court, where procedures are more formal and penalties more severe. In some cases, children as young as ten have been transferred from juvenile to adult court. Lawmakers at both the federal and state level have set mandatory sentences for juvenile offenses.

Many observers believe that the rights of children in the juvenile justice system are not being adequately protected forty years after the Gault decision. Some critics think that the juvenile justice system should be abolished completely. Others argue that children are not adults and their needs cannot be met in adult courts. They acknowledge that juvenile courts may not be the answer for some youthful offenders who continually break the law or who commit the most serious crimes. But, they say, juvenile courts benefit both troubled youths and society by focusing not only on rights but on rehabilitation for young offenders who can be helped to turn away from a life of crime.

GERALD GAULT, CENTER, IS SHOWN ON MAY 16, 1967, ON THE DAY AFTER THE U.S. SUPREME COURT RULED IN HIS FAVOR. HE WAS STUDYING AUTOMOTIVE AND HEAVY EQUIPMENT OPERATION AT THE PARKS JOB CORPS CENTER NEAR PLEASANTON, CALIFORNIA IN 1967.

one
"DELINQUENT CHILD"

THE MORNING OF JUNE 8, 1964, began as a typical late-spring day for Gerald Francis Gault. The fifteen-year-old eighth-grader planned to start his first job that day, distributing flyers for a local music supplier. His friend, Ronald Lewis, had stopped by, and the two boys were hanging out at Gerald's house in the mobile home park in Globe, Arizona, where they both lived. Gerald's parents were at work, and his older brother, Louis, had left the house.

At 10 a.m., a deputy knocked on the Gaults' door. He told the boys that a neighbor, Ora Cook, had complained to the sheriff's office about obscene phone calls she had received. She believed that Gerald and Ronald had made the calls, according to the sheriff. According to later reports, the caller asked Cook questions that she considered lewd: "Do you give any?" "Are your cherries ripe today?" and "Do you have big bombers?"

The sheriff said the boys would have to come with him. He drove them to the Children's Detention Home in Gila County. The sheriff left no word for Gerald's parents about their son's whereabouts, and officials at the detention center did not allow Gerald to call anyone.

Gerald had been in trouble before. Earlier that year,

in February, he had been sentenced to six months' probation because he had been with another boy who had stolen a woman's wallet. Under the terms of his probation, Gerald was supposed to stay out of trouble and obey his mother. The deputy probation officer, Charles Flagg, also happened to be the superintendent of the detention center. He held Gerald in custody until a hearing scheduled the following day.

When Gerald's mother, Marjorie Gault, returned home from work, she had no idea where Gerald was. She sent her older son, Louis, to look for "Jerry," the nickname used by the family. Louis went to Ronald Lewis's home, where he learned what had happened. Police never filed formal charges against Ronald, whose father was a reserve policeman. Gerald said later that Ronald went to live with his mother in California after the incident.

As soon as she learned that Gerald had been taken to the detention center, Marjorie Gault spoke with officials there, who told her the details of the case. She asked whether Gerald needed a lawyer, but her landlord, Rod Weinberger, who was the town's chief of police, told her an attorney was not necessary.

before the judge

The next day, June 9, 1964, Marjorie and her son Louis Gault arrived at the Juvenile Court of Gila County for Gerald's 3 p.m. hearing. His father, Paul Gault, who had just started working for the state at the Grand Canyon more than three hundred miles away, did not accompany them. Juvenile Judge Robert McGhee presided over the informal hearing. Charles Flagg and Ralph Henderson, the probation officers in the case, also attended. Ora Cook, whose complaint began the action against Gerald, was not in court.

Because the session involved a juvenile, no one was

sworn in and the proceedings were not recorded. Those attending remembered the hearing differently. According to the Gaults, Gerald told the judge he had dialed Cook's number but had then handed the telephone over to Ronald. Officer Flagg later recalled that Gerald admitted that he had made the obscene phone calls to Cook. In Judge McGhee's version of events, Gerald admitted that he had said one of the lewd comments to Cook.

The hearing ended without any testimony from Cook. Judge McGhee said he would consider Gerald's case and come to a decision. In the meantime, Gerald was returned to the detention home, where he had been held since the sheriff delivered him there.

On June 11 or June 12—no one is sure which day—officials released Gerald and drove him to the home where Marjorie Gault worked as a babysitter. One of the children called, "Gerald's here." No one explained why he had been released.

Shortly after the hearing, Flagg sent the Gaults a brief message notifying them that on June 15 Judge McGhee would hold "further hearings on Gerald's delinquency." Concerned over the ominous-sounding note, Gerald's father left his job to support his son at the second hearing. As before, Judge McGhee, Flagg, and Henderson appeared at the court. Gerald and his parents and Ronald Lewis and his father also attended. Again, the session was not recorded.

This time, however, both Flagg and the Gaults recalled that Gerald did not admit that he had made the lewd telephone calls. Flagg said that Ronald and Gerald accused each other of the deed while they were being held at the detention center.

Judge McGhee later told the Arizona Superior Court that Gerald had made "some admission again of some of the lewd statements. He didn't admit any of the more serious statements." According to the judge, Gerald admitted that he had made "silly" or "funny calls" to other people in the past.

At one point in the hearing, Marjorie Gault asked that Cook be brought in to identify which of the boys made the calls. The judge denied the request, saying that the law did not require complainants to appear at juvenile hearings. In fact, Flagg was the only official who had spoken to Cook about the matter, and that occurred when she telephoned the sheriff to report the incident. No one at the court or in the sheriff's department had spoken to the woman in person.

The probation officers submitted a report on Gerald's past behavior to the judge. The Gaults did not receive a copy of the report. It contained information about an incident reported two years earlier in which Gerald was accused of stealing a baseball glove and lying to the police department about it. Police apparently did not have enough evidence to charge Gerald, and the matter was dropped without a hearing.

At the conclusion of the hearing, Judge McGhee ruled that Gerald was "a delinquent child." Arizona's juvenile code defined a "delinquent child" as one who:

• violated an ordinance or law;
• was "incorrigible, wayward or habitually disobedient" so that the parents could not control him or her;
• skipped school or ran away from home on a regular basis; or
• "habitually behaves to injure or endanger the morals or health of self or others."

In testimony before the Superior Court, Judge McGhee said he had decided Gerald was "habitually involved in immoral matters" and therefore a "delinquent child" based, in part, on the baseball glove incident.

McGhee sentenced Gerald to the Fort Grant Industrial School, a reform school, until his twenty-first birthday, a period of six years. If an adult had committed the crime— a misdemeanor—the stiffest sentence would have been two months in jail or a fifty-dollar fine.

Later, during a speech at an American Bar Association function, Gerald Gault admitted that he had no idea what was going on in court until the judge issued the sentence and he realized he would be imprisoned for "more years than [I] could count on the fingers of one hand."

As the officers hauled Gerald away, his shocked mother reached out to give her son a good-bye hug, but the judge would not allow it. That indignity, she later told her attorney, led her to seek justice for her son. Eventually, after a three-year court fight, Gerald's case would come before the U.S. Supreme Court and his name would forever be linked to one of the nation's landmark legal decisions.

A wood engraving shows a six-year-old child begging for mercy after being sentenced to the House of Refuge in New York City on a vagrancy charge. Nineteenth-century society meted out harsh punishment for wayward children.

TWO
A COURT FOR JUVENILES

In colonial days, the American legal system did not consider children to be citizens. Until they were on their own, children lived under the control of their father. Parents and the church taught children society's moral codes, but the father ruled over his offspring's lives. He decided what chores they must do and how and when they would be disciplined for misbehavior.

Even so, local officials intervened when they believed fathers were neglecting their duty—either as care provider or as disciplinarian. In one early case, selectmen in Watertown, Massachusetts, ordered a poor family to give their children to others because the children were not receiving proper care. In another case, officials sentenced a boy and his sister to whippings and ordered the local constable to oversee the punishment.

Massachusetts Bay Colony, under the stern direction of the Puritans, meted out harsh punishment to youngsters who did not conform to the settlement's rules. A 1646 statute known as the "stubborn child law" authorized parents to bring their "stubborn or rebellious" sons to court. Children over sixteen could be put to death for cursing or striking their mother or father, although there is no record that officials resorted to such extreme punishment.

THE STATE AS PARENT

The Puritans believed that the state had the right to act as parents of all children living within its jurisdiction. This concept, called *parens patriae* from the Latin words meaning "parent of the country," allowed the state to override parents' authority. The state, under this policy, had the right to intercede when it was in the best interests of the child. Juvenile courts would later assume this role in their dealings with wayward youth.

Colonial law, and later U.S. law, treated children seven years old and older much the same as adults. Their punishment for misdeeds could be severe. In the mid-1800s, for example, a New Jersey court sentenced a twelve-year-old boy to death by hanging for murdering a woman. The state carried out the death sentence, which was "all very constitutional" at the time. Many children served long jail sentences in prisons filled with hardened adult criminals.

Such stiff penalties for children disturbed some Americans. Followers of the English philosopher John Locke believed wayward children could be "re-formed" by taking them out of bad homes and reeducating them in institutions for troubled youth. The New York Society for the Reformation of Juvenile Delinquents, led by New York lawyer James W. Gerard and others, opened the nation's first reform school for children in 1825. Called the New York House of Refuge, the school required its young charges to obey strict rules and remain silent throughout most of the day. The school's regimen focused on prayer, work, and study. According to the founders, "young offender[s]" were to "be subdued with kindness" whenever possible. Despite that edict, youths often endured brutality from their so-called benefactors. School officials whipped misbehaving children, put them in leg irons, and threw them into solitary confinement.

By the end of the decade, Boston and Philadelphia had established their own institutions for delinquent and homeless children. Youthful residents were supposed to learn a trade, but often the children ended up working on local assembly lines at dead-end jobs.

As the Industrial Revolution spread, factories multiplied and jobs beckoned farm workers to the nation's cities. This migration to urban centers began to change the role of children in mid-nineteenth-century America. No longer needed to help on the farm, children in urban families—some as young as six years old—filled jobs at factories seeking cheap labor. Other children, left alone while their parents worked away from home, begged in the streets to try to supplement the family's income. Others ran away to escape harsh treatment on the job or at home. Fathers and a growing number of mothers worked long hours and had little time to participate in their children's education and discipline. The Puritans, who once had overseen children's behavior with a firm hand, no longer controlled communities.

With the loosening of religious and social controls, the state began to expand its role in supervising children. Boston's mayor, an alderman, and the overseers of the poor in that city all had the power to recommend which children should be removed from their families and placed in the House of Refuge. Boys could be kept there until their twenty-first birthday. Girls had to be released at age eighteen. Many of these children had never committed crimes. A judge could put a child in a reform school merely for "idleness," "incorrigibility," "mischievous propensities," or "associating with vicious persons." Parents could arrange to have their children committed for no reason at all.

In 1831 the case of *Commonwealth* v. *M'Keagy* became one of the first to question the state's power to commit youths to reform schools. The case involved a Pennsylvania boy, Lewis L. Joseph, who had been committed to the Philadelphia House of Refuge for being "an idle and disorderly person." During the committal proceeding, young Lewis's father testified against him. After the boy filed a petition for a writ of habeas corpus, the Court of Common Pleas in Philadelphia ordered the boy's release. The court found that the boy had broken no law: he was not a vagrant and his father was not poor. While allowing the reform school to retain the power to commit juveniles, the court ruled that the reasons for commitment must be based on law. Idleness, the court declared, was not a good enough reason to deprive a youngster of freedom.

> It is when the law is attempted to be applied to subjects who are not vagrants in the just and legal acceptation of the term; . . . that doubts are started and difficulties arise, which often involve the most solemn questions of individual and constitutional rights.

Another Pennsylvania case, in 1839, confirmed the state's right to commit juveniles to reform schools. The case, *Ex parte Crouse*, addressed the committal of a teenage girl, Mary Ann Crouse, to a house of refuge. She sought release on the grounds that the state had violated her constitutional rights by committing her to the institution. The Pennsylvania Supreme Court eventually ruled the house of refuge was a school, not a prison. According to the ruling, the state had acted as a caring parent, a role the juvenile justice system continued to claim more than a century later. "The infant has been snatched from a course which must have ended in confirmed depravity," the court declared, "and not only is the restraint of her person lawful, but it would be an act of extreme cruelty to release her from it."

SAVING TROUBLED YOUTHS

As the century progressed, states opened more and more reform schools to handle the growing number of problem children. The schools did little, however, to solve the mounting juvenile crime problem. New York City Police Chief George W. Matsell reported in October 1849 that officers had to deal with "constantly increasing numbers of vagrant, idle, and vicious children." According to his estimates, three thousand children roamed New York streets. The chief predicted they would soon join a "ceaseless stream" of criminals in local jails and state prisons.

Others offered a far higher estimate: according to child advocates of the time, about thirty thousand homeless children lived on the streets of New York. Alarmed at the huge numbers of poor children and the desperate conditions under which they lived, Charles Loring Brace founded the New York Children's Aid Society in 1853. During its first year, the society opened an industrial school for homeless and neglected children. The organization also began the Orphan Train Movement that year, which placed orphaned and homeless children from New York with farmers in the Midwest and West. The controversial program, which placed 120,000 youngsters over the next fifty years, later became a model for the foster parent system.

Brace believed that homeless youngsters could be rescued from the streets and a grim future by putting them under the care and supervision of "morally upright" farm families. The society later opened an industrial school for troubled boys. Established in 1864, the school served as a refuge for boys whom others regarded as "petty thieves, pickpockets, little peddlers, street boys, and young roughs of all ages."

In the late 1800s, those who shared Brace's philosophy promoted the idea that troubled youths could be saved if they were given the proper guidance and conditions. The years between 1890 and 1920 became known as the Progressive Era. The Progressives believed that children were innately good and that society should be more responsive to their needs. Professional psychologists, many of whom worked with children, added their voices to the call for a different approach in dealing with wayward youth.

Since colonial times, children had been tried in adult courts. Many served time in jails with adult criminals. During the 1890s British reporter William T. Stead wrote sensational accounts of young offenders forced by adult prisoners to act as messengers in Chicago jails. The stories shocked the public and led officials to set up a separate school for boys in the Cook County House of Correction. The Chicago Woman's Club pushed for a separate court for juveniles, and in July 1899 the Illinois legislature passed the Juvenile Court Law, establishing the nation's first juvenile court. The juvenile court had broad powers to order treatment for offenders under age sixteen. It had the authority to take youths from their homes, place them in institutions, or put them on probation. In establishing the juvenile court, the legislature intended to "create a flexible, active institution that would function (so it was hoped) in the best interests of the child."

Child advocates throughout the nation worked to establish separate juvenile courts in their areas. In Denver, Judge Benjamin Lindsey led the effort in Colorado to focus on treatment rather than imprisonment when dealing with youthful offenders. The judge had presided over a trial in 1899 of a young boy convicted of stealing coal. After the trial, Lindsey visited the boy's family, poor immigrants living in poverty. When he saw the conditions the boy lived in, Lindsey concluded he was "not a criminal, not a bad boy, merely a boy."

By 1925, forty-six states had established separate courts for juveniles. The focus of the juvenile courts lay on rehabilitating rather than punishing young offenders. Proceedings were conducted under civil code, rather than as criminal trials. To protect the child, hearings were private and the records sealed so that the youngster would not be branded as a criminal. The court did not charge youths with specific crimes; instead they classified them as delinquents. In many jurisdictions, court proceedings were informal events held in the judge's chambers or conducted by probation officers. Often a troubled youth and his or her parents met alone with the judge and the probation officers assigned to the case. Proponents of the juvenile justice system believed that the presence of an attorney would disrupt the informal proceedings, making the state an adversary rather than a cooperative partner in helping the child.

After reviewing young offenders' backgrounds, judges called on social workers and other professionals to help design treatment programs for individual youths. The system allowed judges to order a wide variety of treatments: vocational training, education, hospital care, jail, and probation were among the options. Many child experts believed a child would stop behaving like a criminal if the court followed the right formula in his or her treatment program.

problems mount

From the beginning, juvenile courts were overburdened with cases. The situation became worse during the Depression of the 1930s. More than 250,000 children roamed the streets in search of shelter and food. Police arrested many of them for vagrancy, and their cases clogged the nation's juvenile courts.

Other problems beset the new court system. Most

juvenile judges had no training in childhood development and treatment. While some relied on child experts
for advice, many others based decisions on their own
personal values. According to the National Crime Commission, one-half of the nation's juvenile judges serving
in 1964 did not have college degrees. Many were political
appointees with no experience dealing with children.

In addition, many treatment centers lacked even
basic educational programs. The worst centers subjected
their young charges to brutal whippings, as revealed in a
study conducted at St. Charles School in the late 1920s by
the Illinois Crime Commission.

Perhaps the worst indictment of the juvenile justice
system was that it did not work. Juvenile crime rates continued to soar. Despite receiving so-called treatment,
young offenders returned to the court for new offenses. In
1965 more than half the youths serving time in reform
schools in Washington, D.C., had been there before.

Critics took aim at the system, arguing that judges
had too much power, while youngsters and their parents
lacked even the protections offered hardened adult
defendants. Even so, child advocates did not focus seri-
ously on the rights of young offenders until the 1960s
during the push for civil rights. In 1960 volunteer lawyers
in the Legal Aid Society conducted a study in New York to
see if youngsters would benefit from having their own
lawyers during juvenile proceedings. The study showed
that children rarely understood what was going on during
the proceedings without the help of a lawyer. As a result
of the study, New York legislators passed the Family
Court Act of 1962. The act abolished the old juvenile
court system and set up a family court with lawyers for
young offenders who had no counsel of their own.

Other states, however, resisted following New York's
lead. Many juvenile court judges particularly objected to

JOSEPH E. RAGEN, SEATED, WARDEN AT A CHICAGO PENITENTIARY, DESCRIBES
PRISON LIFE TO NINE MEMBERS OF A TEENAGE GANG CONVICTED IN A FATAL
SHOOTING IN 1956.

the presence of lawyers, whom they believed pitted the
child against court officials. The judges argued that
lawyers prevented them from talking with youngsters and
probing what lay behind the child's actions. Without that
information, judges said they could not determine the
best treatment for the child.

test case

In 1965 about one-fifth of those arrested for serious crimes were under eighteen. Juveniles accounted for more than half of the arrests for serious property offenses. That year 601,000 youths appeared in juvenile court. With that many cases being handled annually, it was just a matter of time before one came before the U.S. Supreme Court.

The case involved Morris A. Kent, a sixteen-year-old boy from Washington, D.C., who had been arrested and charged with breaking into a house, stealing the wallet of the woman who lived there, and raping her. Morris had been under the supervision of the juvenile court system for two years, since he had been apprehended for other break-ins at age fourteen. Police officers took him into custody following the more recent break-in. They interrogated him for seven hours at police headquarters. After spending the night at the Receiving Home for Children, Morris was returned to the police station, where officers continued to question him. Later that day, his mother hired a lawyer. Psychological tests ordered by the lawyer showed that Morris was "a victim of severe psychopathology." The lawyer filed motions with the juvenile court for a hearing and asked that Morris be hospitalized and treated.

The juvenile judge ruled that Morris should be transferred to criminal court and tried as an adult. Juvenile judges had the power to decide whether cases involving youths should remain in juvenile court or be moved to adult court. In making his ruling, the judge did not consider the motions, did not take into account the psychological tests, and did not hold a hearing. He gave no reasons for his decision and did not even talk with Morris or his lawyer. The judge did not release the boy's files to his lawyer as requested.

The U.S. District Court for the District of Columbia denied Morris's appeal of the transfer. After a jury trial, he was found guilty on six counts of housebreaking and robbery and sentenced to thirty to ninety years in prison. The jury also found him not guilty by reason of insanity on the rape charge. As a result, the court ordered Morris to be taken to a mental institution until his sanity returned. He then would have to serve the remaining jail sentence for the other charges.

Morris's lawyer appealed, and eventually the case made its way to the Supreme Court. The lawyer argued that officers and the juvenile court had violated Morris's rights in several ways:

· Police did not notify Morris's parents of his detention.

· Officials held the boy in custody for about a week without charges or a determination of probable cause.

· Police questioned him without a parent or lawyer present.

· Authorities never told Morris he had a right to remain silent and a right to an attorney.

· He was unlawfully fingerprinted and the evidence was used against him in district court.

Critics of the juvenile court system followed the case closely. They hoped the Court would use *Kent* v. *United States* to lay down firm guidelines to protect the rights of juveniles. Although the Court ruled in Morris's favor, overturning the lower court decision, the ruling was a narrow one. By a close 5 to 4 vote, the Court ruled that the order transferring Morris's case to adult court was invalid. Justice Abe Fortas, who wrote the decision, said that the juvenile court proceedings did not "satisfy the basic requirements of due process and fairness" and did not lead to a "full investigation" of the case as required by law. Fortas acknowledged that the law allowed the juvenile court wide discretion in deciding what should be done with youthful offenders. But, Fortas noted, that did not mean the court could ignore well-established procedures. "[T]here is no place in our system of law for reaching a result of such tremendous consequences without ceremony—without hearing, without effective assistance of counsel, without a statement of reasons."

The Court ordered that a hearing be held on Morris Kent's transfer to adult court. Fortas's ruling did not make any judgment on whether or not Kent's case should be transferred; that decision remained in the hands of the lower courts.

In his opinion, Fortas noted that it would be "extraordinary" if courts allowed children to be treated in a manner that would be unacceptable in an adult court. Morris's case, he said, raised a number of "disturbing" questions about how police and the juvenile court in the District of Columbia dealt with juvenile offenders. He pointed to evidence that some juvenile courts, including the D.C. court, lacked the personnel, the facilities, and the techniques to provide adequate treatment to troubled youth. "There is evidence, in fact, that there may be grounds for concern that the child receives the worst of both worlds: that he gets neither the protections accorded to adults nor the solicitous care and regenerative treatment postulated for children," Fortas wrote.

Nevertheless, Fortas resisted pressure to use the *Kent* case to extend to children the constitutional protections that applied to adults. He went no further than ruling on the specific case; the decision laid down no further guidelines for the juvenile court. As it turned out, *In re Gault* would have much more impact on the nation's juvenile courts than the *Kent* case.

THree
SEEKING JUSTICE

ARIZONA, LIKE many states in the 1960s, did not allow defendants in juvenile cases to appeal a judge's order. Desperate to free their son, the Gaults called the Arizona attorney general's office to see what could be done. Officials there suggested the family contact Amelia Dietrich Lewis, a well-known Arizona attorney in Sun City who was affiliated with the Arizona chapter of the American Civil Liberties Union (ACLU). The ACLU, a nonprofit organization founded in 1920, had long been a champion of civil rights.

Marjorie Gault told Lewis about her son's predicament and said she did not consider him a delinquent. Gerald, she later testified, "is an obedient boy who has gotten into some trouble, not of a serious enough nature for the punishment meted out to him."

Lewis agreed to take the case. She said later that she decided to take Gerald Gault's case because "I have raised three healthy sons, and I wanted to give something back." Since the law barred an appeal, the lawyer filed a petition for a writ of habeas corpus to free Gerald. The term habeas corpus is Latin, literally meaning "you shall have the body." A writ of habeas corpus asks that a prisoner be brought to court for a hearing to determine

AMELIA LEWIS, THE ARIZONA LAWYER WHO REPRESENTED GERALD GAULT IN
THE INITIAL STAGES OF HIS COURT FIGHT.

whether officials followed legal procedures when detaining him or her. It provides a legal shield against the abuse of power by leaders who would imprison opponents illegally. A person petitioning for such a writ must show that officials made an error in ordering the imprisonment.

CENTERPIECE OF LIBERTY

The writ of habeas corpus has been called "one of the centerpieces of our liberties" and is seen as an important tool in safeguarding the freedom of individuals against lawless officials. In 1679, under pressure from the public, the English Parliament adopted the Habeas Corpus Act to prevent officials from illegally imprisoning citizens. America's founders incorporated the right into the U.S. Constitution's Article 1, which states: "The Privilege of the Writ of Habeas Corpus shall not be suspended, unless when in Cases of Rebellion or Invasion the public Safety may require it." State constitutions also guarantee the right of prisoners to petition for a writ of habeas corpus.

Under habeas corpus, people cannot be jailed "without due process of law" and without specified charges, the services of a lawyer, and a jury trial. These rights are guaranteed by the Fifth Amendment (in its due process clause) and the Sixth Amendment. The due process clause requires officials to follow legal procedures before depriving a citizen of life or liberty.

In Lewis's petition for habeas corpus, she argued that Gerald had been committed illegally because he had not had a real hearing with a lawyer to argue his case. Lewis also noted that the court had denied her client the opportunity to cross-examine the witnesses against him. Lewis filed the petition with the Arizona Supreme Court, which referred the matter to the state superior court for review. The court scheduled a hearing on Gerald's case to be held August 17, 1964.

Lewis's petition challenged long-standing practice followed in most juvenile cases. For more than sixty years, juvenile courts had operated much differently from adult courts. Hearings were informal, and strict rules of law that required access to lawyers, cross-examination of witnesses, and protection from self-incrimination did not apply to juveniles accused of offenses. In some instances, officials did not even charge juveniles with specific crimes; they accused youngsters merely of being "delinquent." Lawyers rarely got involved with the process at all. Even fewer lawyers challenged the authority of juvenile court judges to determine the fate of young offenders. Those who did protest got nowhere.

With the odds heavily against them, Lewis prepared Gerald's case while the Gaults waited anxiously for a decision they hoped would win their son's freedom. On the day of the hearing, the superior court listened as Judge Robert McGhee described the earlier proceedings against Gerald. When asked what law he had based the sentence on, Judge McGhee replied:

> I think it amounts to disturbing the peace. I can't give you the section, but I can tell you the law, that when one person uses lewd language in the presence of another person . . . and I consider that when a person makes it over the phone, that it is considered in the presence, I might be wrong, that is one section. The other section upon which I consider the boy delinquent is Section 8-201, Subsection (d), habitually involved in immoral matters.

McGhee, the major witness during the hearing, told the court he considered Gerald to be "involved in immoral matters" based on the baseball glove incident and the fact that the defendant was on probation for another misdeed. Ora Cook, the neighbor who had lodged the original complaint against Gerald, did not attend the hearing.

APPealING THe DeCISIon

The superior court, not unexpectedly, denied the writ. Undeterred, Lewis took the case to the Arizona Supreme Court. She charged that the law cited by Judge McGhee, Section 8-201, violated Gerald's rights because it did not require that Gerald or his parents be given formal notice of a hearing and it did not specify the charges against the boy. In addition, Lewis claimed, the juvenile court proceedings infringed on her client's right to due process because officials did not tell him he could have a lawyer or that he did not have to discuss the charges against him.

In her arguments to the state supreme court, Lewis noted other failings in the juvenile proceedings. For one, the lack of a written record made it difficult to determine whether proper procedure had been followed. Cook, the complainant, had never been sworn in and had not testified in court. In adult courts, a defendant has a right to face his accusers and hear what they have to say. Hearsay testimony—statements made by a person reporting what someone else has said—are not allowed in an adult court. Witnesses there must testify in person. Lewis also told the court that no one had ever determined that the Gaults were unfit parents or that Gerald should be taken away from their care.

Lewis's arguments did not convince the Arizona Supreme Court. On November 10, 1965, the court rejected Gerald's appeal. In making its decision, the court reconfirmed the role of the juvenile court as protector of youthful offenders and put its control firmly in the hands of the presiding judge. "Juvenile courts do not exist to punish children for their transgressions against society," the court noted in its ruling. "The juvenile court stands in the position of a protecting parent rather than a prosecutor. . . . The aim of the [juvenile] court is to provide individualized justice for children."

In addition, the supreme court endorsed many of the methods criticized by Lewis. Juvenile systems had to be flexible, the court noted, to be able to deal with each child's individual needs. The judge could decide whether a transcript should be kept of the proceedings. Transcripts were used to keep a record of the proceedings for use in an appeal, but since juvenile courts did not allow appeals, no transcript was required. The judge could also decide whether to allow a youth to be represented by an attorney.

Hearsay evidence could be used in juvenile proceedings if it was "of a kind on which reasonable men are accustomed to rely in serious affairs," according to the supreme court. None of these methods, the court contended, violated the Constitution, as Lewis claimed. The ruling noted:

> All jurisdictions have juvenile codes and all provide for less than the full set of due process guarantees available in a criminal proceeding. Yet, the overwhelming majority of courts have expressly or impliedly recognized the statutes to be constitutional.

In Gerald's case, the court ruled, Judge McGhee had conducted the proceedings according to the law. The Gaults had been told of the hearing, were well aware of the charges against Gerald, and had attended the hearing without objection. The supreme court also noted that the Gaults had been told by Judge McGhee during the earlier hearing in February that Gerald could be sent to the juvenile home if he got into trouble again.

Gerald's Release

The state supreme court's dismissal of Gerald's appeal made Lewis even more determined to pursue his case. She vowed to take it all the way to the U.S. Supreme Court if necessary. A formidable lawyer who had worked in the juvenile justice system for decades, Lewis had many times overcome what others might have considered insurmountable odds. She had been born in the Bronx, a borough of New York City, and had earned a law degree from St. Lawrence University's law school in New York. During the 1920s and 1930s, the school became known for its open-door policy, admitting poor students, blacks, and women who were barred by other schools because of discriminatory policies.

One of the few women to be admitted to the New York bar in the early 1920s, Lewis worked as a lawyer in New York City's juvenile justice system for thirty-three years. In 1957, after the death of her husband, she moved to Arizona and took the bar exam there. She was one of two women taking the exam that day. The other woman— Sandra Day O'Connor—went on to become the first woman justice appointed to the U.S. Supreme Court, in 1981. Lewis practiced law until two years before her death in 1994 at the age of ninety-one.

By the time the Arizona State Supreme Court issued its opinion in the Gault case, the state had released Gerald from Fort Grant. He served 179 days at the school, during which he chopped weeds out of rows of cotton, a job that began at "the crack of dawn" and earned him $1.60 a day. "It was hell," Gerald said of the experience during an interview years later. The other inmates had committed crimes ranging from petty theft to murder, Gault said. He received no job training and no counseling during his stay at the school. No one ever explained to him why the state decided to release him, he said. "They just let me go."

Gerald Gault: "A Good Kid in the Wrong Place"

Gerald Gault first heard of the Supreme Court's decision in his case from a local news reporter who came to the Job Corps Center in Pleasanton, California, where he was studying welding and automotive and heavy equipment operation. He recalled that he became a celebrity "for fifteen to twenty minutes" for his role as the central figure in the case.

Gault later married, had two sons, and became a successful computer technician. He said he considered the case "an unfortunate thing that happened back then. It surely didn't benefit me." It did, however, affect his life and the lives of his family. Gerald's father, Paul, worked as a miner; his mother, Marjorie, cared for other people's children for a living. The family had little money. Paul Gault, who had started a state job at the Grand Canyon two weeks before the incident that led to the case, had to leave the job to come home and help his son with his legal difficulties. "We're a family that sticks together," Gerald Gault said later.

At each new stage of the case, whenever news reports appeared in the local paper, Gerald suffered the consequences. "It stopped me from getting jobs," he recalled. "Something would come up in the paper, and people would say, 'You're a juvenile delinquent. We don't want you.'"

Known to his family as "Jerry," the young Gault served time at the state reform school after the juvenile judge declared him a delinquent. His lawyer, Amelia Lewis, called him "a good kid in the wrong place at the wrong time." Years later, she told a news reporter that Gault still sent her a card every Christmas. Gault rarely makes public appearances in connection with the landmark decision, but in 1987 he attended an American Bar Association event at which Amelia Lewis received an award for her work on the case. The ceremony was part of a celebration marking the twentieth anniversary of the Gault decision.

After being released from Fort Grant, Gerald, an eighth-grader at the time of his commitment, went back to school. He eventually dropped out, worked on a ranch, and studied welding at the Job Corps. After a short stint at a junior college (where he admitted he "goofed off"), Gault joined the Army in 1969. He became a cook and served in Korea. When his tour of duty ended, he left the Army and married. Later he rejoined the Army and served from 1973 to 1991, working in Germany twice, first in the infantry and then in charge of the motor pool. He ended his Army career as a sergeant after traveling to countries all over the world.

Though he did not benefit from the Supreme Court case himself, Gault believes others did. "The children of the U.S. definitely benefited by it, and that's good," he said. He has mixed feelings about the state of the juvenile justice system after the Gault decision, though. Because of the case, juveniles have well-established rights, Gault said. He notes, however, that several states have since passed laws allowing young teenagers to be tried as adults, a trend he views as harmful to juveniles. "Fourteen years old—that's still a child," he said.

ASSOCIATE JUSTICE SANDRA DAY O'CONNOR DURING CONFIRMATION HEAR-
INGS ON SEPTEMBER 9, 1961. SHE AND GERALD GAULT'S ATTORNEY, AMELIA
LEWIS, TOOK THE ARIZONA BAR EXAM ON THE SAME DAY. O'CONNOR WOULD
LATER SERVE ON THE COURT THAT RULED ON THE *IN RE GAULT* CASE.

Frank Lewis, who followed his mother's work on Gault's case, surmised that the state hoped the Gaults would drop the case if Gerald was released. Overcrowding at the school and pressure to release juveniles there on minor charges provided another incentive to free Gerald, Lewis said. Judge McGhee, who might have opposed Gerald's release, had been removed from the case after testifying as a witness at the habeas corpus proceeding.

PETITIONING THE U.S. SUPREME COURT

Whatever the reason for Gerald's release, it did not change Amelia Lewis's determination to pursue the case. She contacted Norman Dorsen, a noted civil rights attorney and law professor at New York University's School of Law, for help in preparing an appeal to the U.S. Supreme Court. Dorsen, a former classmate of Frank Lewis, was a leader in the American Civil Liberties Union campaign to protect constitutional rights. He later served as ACLU general counsel and president.

Lewis's call intrigued Dorsen. He said in an interview years later, "It sounded very interesting." He agreed to work on the appeal. Although he would spend more than a year on the appeal and would be linked to the landmark case forever, Dorsen said he did not remember ever meeting Gerald. The lawyer's work revolved around the constitutional issues involved in the case and the way juvenile courts were run. In fact, the case that Dorsen presented to the Supreme Court had much more to do with the Fourteenth Amendment than with Gerald himself. The ACLU agreed to foot the bill for the costly Court battle. On the last day of the Court session in late June 1966, Dorsen filed a petition asking the Court to review *In re Gault*.

Norman Dorsen, a leader in the American Civil Liberties Union, argued Gerald Gault's case before the U.S. Supreme Court.

four
STATING THE CASE

Norman Dorsen knew that to win a spot on the Supreme Court's docket, a case had to raise vital issues that set it apart from the thousands of other cases vying for a hearing. Each year more than nine thousand appellants seek a review by the nation's high court. Only a small fraction—fewer than one hundred cases—attract the Court's attention.

The nine justices hear cases from October until late June or early July. Each Friday the justices meet to discuss cases before them and to set the schedule for the upcoming session. Usually the chief justice prepares a list of the cases he considers to be the most important. Occasionally, associate justices will add cases to the list as well. After a discussion—sometimes spirited—the justices vote on the cases they will hear. To be considered by the Court, a case must win the votes of at least four justices. The justices do not vote on the case itself; only on whether it merits a review by the Court.

Dorsen, like most people who seek a hearing before the Supreme Court, submitted a petition for *certiorari*. Such a petition is a formal request that the case be moved from a lower court to a higher court. *Certiorari* means "to be informed of." If the petition is granted, the record of the previous hearing or trial is then sent to the higher court for review (so the court will be "informed" of the proceedings).

The petition outlines the facts of the case and states the reasons why the Court should consider it. As the highest court in the land, the U.S. Supreme Court reviews only cases that deal with matters of great importance. Its decisions influence rulings in all other U.S. courts and lay the groundwork for future Court rulings. To be heard, a case usually must deal with one of three issues:

- constitutional rights or questions;
- a conflict between rulings of different courts;
- a decision by a state court on a federal law.

In preparing his petition, Dorsen focused on the constitutional issues raised by the Gault case. He argued that the Constitution guaranteed certain rights, including the right to due process, to juveniles as well as to adults. The petition claimed that the courts of Arizona had deprived Gerald Gault of these rights.

Initially it seemed that the Court would not hear Gerald's appeal. Earlier that spring, the justices had scheduled a similar case for oral argument that legal experts believed would decide the future of the juvenile court system. After reviewing the Gault case, however, the Court dismissed the other juvenile case and scheduled *In re Gault* instead, presumably because the justices believed Gerald Gault's petition presented the issues more clearly. The lawyers would argue the case before the Court on December 6, 1966.

Officially known as No. 116, In the matter of the Application of Paul L. Gault and Marjorie Gault, father and mother of Gerald Francis Gault, a minor, appellants, the case became *In re Gault* in its shortened form. *In re,* a legal term meaning "in the matter of," is used in cases where an appellant is asking the Court to take some action on his behalf. In most cases, an appellant opposes another party, as in *Brown* v. *Board of Education*, the famous school desegregation case. In this case, the Gaults had not filed suit against the state or anyone else; they were merely asking the Court to free Gerald. Since the state institution had released Gerald by the time the case came before the Supreme Court, the lawyers focused on the principles involved in the case, rather than a plea to free him. Usually, courts will not hear a case unless the appellant is still involved in the situation being discussed (for example, under arrest or in jail for a crime). In Gerald's case, however, the Court agreed to the appeal because Gerald remained under the jurisdiction of the state institution until he turned twenty-one. In 1966, when the case came before the Court, Gerald was seventeen years old.

Brief for the Appellant

Lawyers for both sides in a case prepare documents in which they describe the events that led to the court action, discuss the issues involved, and detail arguments, supporting evidence, and previous court decisions that bolster their point of view. These documents, called briefs, are usually anything but brief. Judges and justices refer to the briefs when deciding a case, and lawyers want to include every point they can to win the court's support.

Briefs in the Gault case were due in the fall, which would give the justices time to review them before hearing oral arguments. The lawyers worked over the summer to meet the Court's deadline. Dorsen and Lewis, representing Gerald Gault, worked with constitutional law experts Melvin L. Wulf (ACLU general counsel) and Daniel A. Rezneck in preparing their brief. The discussion and arguments ultimately filled sixty-three pages, plus a fifteen-page appendix. In the brief, Gault's lawyers focused on two major points:

> • In the course of treating each juvenile offender individually, juvenile courts had done away with traditional legal safeguards that the Constitution guaranteed all citizens. "The barter of due process for individualized treatment has cost juveniles dearly," the brief noted.
> • The Arizona Juvenile Code had not established rules to ensure that juvenile courts treated children fairly. Because of the code's omission of such rules, young suspects were being deprived of the constitutional rights of due process guaranteed by the Fourteenth Amendment. "This deprivation of rights," the brief contended, "cannot be justified."

In supporting Gerald's case, the lawyers argued that the state, in its role as parent, had failed to serve the best interests of the children it sought to protect. "The 'parens patriae' notion is no substitute for the fairness that the juvenile is entitled to when his vital interests are at stake," the brief concluded.

The brief also attacked the argument that juvenile courts differed from adult courts because they conducted civil proceedings, not criminal, and that they offered treatment rather than punishment. Adult courts, the brief noted, frequently provided treatment at mental hospitals and in counseling programs for criminals. And in some cases, the brief continued, youthful offenders were confined in institutions far longer than an adult would be jailed if convicted of the same misdeed.

Dorsen cited New York State's Family Court Act, which had noted the need to protect children's rights. According to the brief, New York as well as several federal and state courts and "scholarly commentators" had recognized "that there are compelling reasons of fairness to provide young people with basic procedural protections in juvenile court."

The brief listed six rights—all of which had been denied Gerald—that were necessary to ensure fair treatment of juveniles:

Adequate notice of the charges. Law officials should be required to tell youths of the charges against them. Without that knowledge, accused youths could not plan their defense. Gerald Gault was not told what law he had violated or the consequences if he were found guilty. He had no idea that the charge could lead to confinement in a state institution for six years.

The right to an attorney. The Supreme Court had already ruled in the 1963 case *Gideon* v. *Wainwright* that adult defendants were entitled to lawyers and that the state had to pay for lawyers for those who could not afford one. In *Miranda* v. *Arizona*, decided in 1966, the Court had required police to warn suspects of their right to an attorney before questioning them. No one had suggested to Gerald that he could have a lawyer represent him during the proceedings.

While juvenile court did not technically sentence youths to prison, many youngsters faced social stigma and the loss of their freedom if a judge declared them to be delinquents.

Young offenders needed a lawyer's help even more than adults did, Dorsen contended. "Legal counsel is particularly vital in juvenile proceedings," he wrote. Children often were too young to understand the proceedings, had no knowledge of legal rights, and could not grasp the effect court actions might have on their future.

AFTER BEING WRONGLY FOUND GUILTY OF BURGLARY, CLARENCE EARL GIDEON CHALLENGED HIS CONVICTION AND WON A VICTORY IN THE U.S. SUPREME COURT. HIS CASE ESTABLISHED THAT ADULTS ACCUSED OF A CRIME WERE ENTITLED TO AN ATTORNEY AND THAT THE STATE HAD TO PAY FOR SUCH SERVICES IF DEFENDANTS COULD NOT AFFORD TO HIRE THEIR OWN ATTORNEYS.

In addition, the brief noted, many juvenile court judges did not have legal training or worked part-time, and it said that even legal experts disagreed on which rights applied to children.

The right to confront and cross-examine witnesses. Youths (or their lawyers) should be able to question those making charges or giving evidence against them. If an accused is not allowed to cross-examine witnesses, Dorsen argued, "there can be no fair or reliable determination of truth." Marjorie Gault had asked the judge to bring Ora Cook to the courtroom to identify the voice of the boy who had made the lewd calls. The judge refused to do so, instead relying on confusing testimony that never really resolved which boy had said the obscene words and what actually happened. The judge himself never spoke with the woman, who did not appear in court for any of the proceedings.

The right against self-incrimination. Dorsen argued that the probation officers and the court had violated the Constitution when it failed to warn Gerald that any statements he made could be used against him and that he did not have to testify. Quoting a 1964 Supreme Court case, *Murphy* v. *Waterfront Commission*, Dorsen noted that the right against self-incrimination can be claimed "in any proceeding, be it criminal or civil, administrative or judicial, investigative or adjudicatory."

The right to a transcript. Without a record of the court proceedings in Gerald's case, the higher courts had to rely on the recollections of the people involved—and they had differing views on what had transpired.

The right to appeal. Arizona law, and the law in many other states at the time, did not allow appeals from juvenile court. Dorsen noted that without an appeals process, the judge in a case had "practically unlimited discretion" over the hearing and how it was run, the criteria used in finding guilt, and the sentencing. Some process of review must be allowed to make certain hearings were conducted fairly, the brief concluded.

Amicus Briefs

Three other briefs filed with the Court supported Gerald Gault's position. These documents, called *amicus curiae* briefs, were filed by the Legal Aid Society and Citizens'

THrOuGH THe COurT SYSTem

First Stop: State Court
Almost all cases (about 95 percent) start in state courts. These courts go by various names, depending on the state in which they operate: circuit, district, municipal, county, or superior. The case is tried and decided by a judge, a panel of judges, or a jury.

The side that loses can then appeal to the next level.

First Stop: Federal Court
U.S. DISTRICT COURT—About 5 percent of cases begin their journey in federal court. Most of these cases concern federal laws, the U.S. Constitution, or disputes that involve two or more states. They are heard in one of the ninety-four U.S. district courts in the nation.
U.S. COURT OF INTERNATIONAL TRADE—Federal court cases involving international trade appear in the U.S. Court of International Trade.
U.S. CLAIMS COURT—The U.S. Claims Court hears federal cases that involve more than $10,000, Indian claims, and some disputes with government contractors.

The loser in federal court can appeal to the next level.

Appeals: State Cases
Forty states have appeals courts that hear cases that have come from the state courts. In states without an appeals court, the case goes directly to the state supreme court.

Appeals: Federal Cases
U.S. CIRCUIT COURT—Cases appealed from U.S. district courts go to U.S. circuit courts of appeals. There are twelve circuit courts that handle cases from throughout the

nation. Each district court and every state and territory are assigned to one of the twelve circuits. Appeals in a few state cases—those that deal with rights guaranteed by the U.S. Constitution—are also heard in this court.

U.S. COURT OF APPEALS—Cases appealed from the U.S. Court of International Trade and the U.S. Claims Court are heard by the U.S. Court of Appeals for the Federal Circuit. Among the cases heard in this court are those involving patents and minor claims against the federal government.

Further Appeals: State Supreme Court

Cases appealed from state appeals courts go to the highest courts in the state—usually called supreme court. In New York, the state's highest court is called the court of appeals. Most state cases do not go beyond this point.

Final Appeals: U.S. Supreme Court

The U.S. Supreme Court is the highest court in the country. Its decision on a case is the final word. The Court decides issues that can affect every person in the nation. It has decided cases on slavery, abortion, school segregation, and many other important issues.

The Court selects the cases it will hear—usually around one hundred each year. Four of the nine justices must vote to consider a case in order for it to be heard. Almost all cases have been appealed from the lower courts (either state or federal).

Most people seeking a decision from the Court submit a petition for certiorari. Certiorari means that the case will be moved from a lower court to a higher court for review. The Court receives about nine thousand of these requests annually. The petition outlines the case and gives reasons why the Court should review it.

In rare cases, for example *New York Times* v. *United States*, an issue must be decided immediately. When such a case is of national importance, the Court allows it to bypass the usual lower court system and hears the case directly.

To win a spot on the Court's docket, a case must fall within one of the following categories:

 • Disputes between states and the federal government or between two or more states. The Court also reviews cases involving ambassadors, consuls, and foreign ministers.

 • Appeals from state courts that have ruled on a federal question.

 • Appeals from federal appeals courts (about two-thirds of all requests fall into this category).

Committee for New York, the National Legal Aid and Defender Association, and the American Parents Committee. The Court often allows outside groups—*amici curiae*, or friends of the court—to file briefs on behalf of one side or the other in a case. Like other briefs, these serve to inform the justices of issues related to the case. The group presenting the *amicus* brief often has a special interest in the topic; in the Gault case, the *amicus* briefs focused on the juvenile court system. On rare occasions (but not in the Gault case), the Court invites the author of an *amicus* brief to present his or her views during oral arguments.

The Legal Aid Society and Citizens' Committee, a nonprofit group that represented poor youth in New York's juvenile court system, argued for "the establishment of the requirements of fair procedure as a matter of constitutional right."

In its twenty-eight-page brief, the group debunked the idea that it was better for juveniles to keep court proceedings secret than to have their constitutional rights protected. The brief questioned whether the court's "policy of hiding 'youthful errors' could justify the uncertainties and confusion in this [Gerald's] proceeding." Juvenile proceedings were so similar "in substance and import" to criminal trials, the brief maintained, that they should observe the same constitutional safeguards.

A juvenile proceeding, according to the brief, involved more than the rights of children. It also involved those of the parents, who had an interest in what happened to their child and a right to his or her custody. Neither Gerald nor his parents knew what factors the judge considered when he ordered Gerald's commitment to the state institution. Had a hearing been required to explore the judge's reasons, the Gaults might have been able to introduce favorable information, dispute erroneous claims, and convince the judge to take another look at the matter. "Nothing less," the brief contended, "can stand as a safeguard against misinformation, misinterpretation, and arbitrariness."

Furthermore, the society argued, the Arizona law on delinquency and conduct "endangering morals or health" was too vague. Because the law did not specify exact behavior, the brief contended, the judge could rule that a child had violated the law based solely on "his personal values and individual interpretation of the statute."

The National Legal Aid and Defender Association focused its arguments on juvenile offenders' right to an attorney. The 1,400-member group included many lawyers nationwide who represented poor clients in juvenile proceedings. The case, the group noted, was "of vital concern to its members" because its outcome would directly affect "the continuing validity" of the members' work in juvenile courts.

Anyone who is facing a loss of liberty is entitled to an attorney, the group argued. "The right of counsel in any proceeding in which personal liberty is at stake is a basic requirement of the Sixth Amendment and the Due Process Clause of the 14th, regardless of the forum," the brief maintained. Among other things, the Sixth Amendment, part of the Bill of Rights, guarantees that anyone charged in a criminal prosecution has the right "to have the assistance of counsel for his defense."

A person's young age should have no effect on his or her right to an attorney, the group argued. Children, it contended, should not be deprived of a lawyer's help when it is available to adults. The brief disputed the Arizona Supreme Court's claim that juveniles did not need the services of a lawyer because "the parent and the probation officer may be relied upon to protect the infant's interests." It noted that Gerald's mother had tried to question Cook without success. And the probation officer, the brief observed, was Gerald's chief accuser, the only prosecution witness to testify against the youth. The NLADA brief concluded with a quote from the *Kent* opinion written by Justice Abe Fortas: "The right to representation by counsel is not a formality. It is not a grudging gesture to a ritualistic requirement. It is of the essence of justice."

A third *amicus* brief on Gerald's behalf was filed by the American Parents Committee. The APC, a nonprofit group that worked for federal legislation that benefited children, had as its members child welfare workers, researchers, educators, and community and business leaders. It joined the case because it believed *Gault* posed "questions which are of great importance to all parents and children, as well as to the American community at large."

In its brief, the APC detailed seven arguments:

1) The safeguards guaranteed in the Constitution are essential in any system with the power to take away a person's freedom.

2) The Constitution does not permit two systems of justice, "one legal and the other extra-legal."

3) The adversary system of justice, where two sides take opposite stands, offers the best guarantee that people will be treated fairly.

4) In addition to protecting their youthful clients, attorneys protect society as a whole by helping ensure that children are not unnecessarily committed to reform schools. As a result, society is spared the related costs—both monetary and in damaged lives. The brief questioned whether Gerald's commitment to Fort Grant would help him or turn him "into a greater public hazard."

5) A legal system that denies children the rights

of citizenship makes it more difficult for them to become responsible citizens as adults.

6) Even though the juvenile court would have to hire more staff and spend more money to ensure that children's rights were met, "these are the expected costs of American justice."

7) Juvenile proceedings should be opened to public view. Operating the juvenile court behind closed doors, the brief contended, raised everyone's suspicions, from those who fought for due process for children to those who believed judges "coddled" young offenders. "After half a century as an unproven social experiment," the brief concluded, "the juvenile process needs to go more into the open and is likely to benefit from the opportunity for a public assessment."

Arizona makes its case

Arizona Assistant Attorney General Frank A. Parks, joined by Attorney General Darrell F. Smith, prepared the state's thirty-two-page brief. Parks's central theme revolved around the view that the state served as a caring parent for troubled youths. It protected them and arranged for treatment that aimed to turn them into productive citizens.

The state's brief portrayed the juvenile court as a place without adversaries, where everyone looked out for the interests of wayward youths. Parks argued that unlike adult courts, those set up for juveniles focused on treatment, not punishment. To bolster his point, Parks quoted from a 1955 Pennsylvania case, *In re Holmes*:

[The juvenile court's] purpose is not penal but protective,—aimed to check juvenile delinquency and to throw around a child, just starting, perhaps,

on an evil course and deprived of proper parental
care, the strong arm of the state. . . . The State is
not seeking to punish an offender but to salvage a
boy who may be in danger of becoming one, and to
safeguard his adolescent life.

Parks contended that the courts treated youths fairly,
but informally. Under such conditions, he noted, the
requirements of due process should be viewed differently
from those of more formal adult courts. To serve juveniles'
needs, he noted, the court tailored each sentence to fit the
particular situation of each youth rather than issue standard sentences based on the offense. To do this, however,
the judge had to be able to talk with the child in trouble and
go over police records and social service reports detailing
his or her circumstances. The court itself was set up to
make the youngster feel at ease. No one stood when the
judge entered the room, and the judge sat at the same level
as the child. In some areas, sessions were held in the
judge's chambers rather than the more formal courtroom.

If juvenile courts were required to adopt the formal
procedures of adult courts, the brief argued, the friendly
atmosphere would disappear. Children would be less
likely to confide in the judge. Such formality, Parks noted,
would make the proceeding adversarial, pitting the judge
and the child against each other. He wrote, "The juvenile
court would be destroyed if injected with the rights of due
process as construed in the criminal system."

Since the juvenile court did not issue criminal sentences, formal procedures were unnecessary, Parks contended. Instead of criminal charges and penalties, the
juvenile court decided on treatment plans based on
the needs of each individual child. The juvenile courts
treated children fairly, according to Parks, and that was
all the Constitution required.

The Arizona juvenile court was a busy place in 1964, the year Gerald appeared before Judge McGhee. According to the brief, the Gila County court held 365 juvenile hearings that year. Judge McGhee presided over all of them. Probate staff handled another 270 juvenile cases that did not go to court. In addition to Gerald, Judge McGhee sent ten other juveniles to Fort Grant in 1964. Cases may have been handled differently for each offender, but the court nevertheless followed due process, Parks contended.

In Gerald's case, he noted, the court conducted a "fair and purposeful hearing." Because Gerald confessed to taking part in the obscene phone calls, the court had no need to examine charges against him. If Gerald had denied having anything to do with the calls, the brief asserted, then he would have been entitled to defend himself in court. As it was, the hearing addressed ways to treat the troubled youth, not convict him.

Parks argued that the Gaults had received adequate notice of both hearings. He pointed out that officer Flagg told Marjorie Gault about the June 9 hearing when she visited Gerald at the detention center. He sent her a written notice about the June 15 hearing. State law did not require the court to warn parents of the outcome of a hearing, according to the brief. In any case, Parks added, Judge McGhee had testified that he told the Gaults at Gerald's February 1964 probation hearing that he could be committed if he returned to the court on another offense.

Due process does not require that children have their own attorneys, the brief noted. Inserting lawyers into juvenile court proceedings would "undermine the informal approach" of the court and transform it into "a junior criminal court," according to the brief. Still, judges had the option of appointing lawyers for young offenders if they believed the children needed legal help. "Such a

FRANK A. PARKS, ARIZONA ASSISTANT ATTORNEY GENERAL, WHO ARGUED FOR THE STATE IN THE *IN RE GAULT* CASE.

tailor-made approach to each individual case," wrote Parks, "would be far more beneficial than a rule absolute." In addition, parents had the right to hire an attorney, if they wished. Parks noted that Marjorie Gault had testified she had considered hiring a lawyer but had decided not to. That proved she was well aware of her right to an attorney.

Parks acknowledged that children and their parents had a right to cross-examine witnesses. In Gerald's case, he noted, there was no need to cross-examine Cook because the boy had already confessed to the acts. The lawyer took issue with another protection available to adults: the right not to incriminate oneself. Judges needed to develop rapport with children in order to help them. To do so, the brief argued, "it is of course essential that the judge encourage [the child] to talk freely." Because the child did not face criminal charges, he or she did not need to be protected against self-incriminating comments. Parks quoted a juvenile judge to make his point:

> The first purpose of a hearing is to learn the truth. Which is the greater justice to the child: to teach him honesty and encourage him to reveal the truth or to pave the way for him to lie and conceal the truth? Doctors diagnose and treat the child whose body is sick. The child is never encouraged to deceive the doctor or to evade his questions. Must there be a different ethic when a child's behavior is sick?

Another adult protection, the right of appeal, was not required in juvenile court to meet the due process standard, the brief noted. Children had no need to appeal what was essentially a treatment program. Furthermore, Parks argued, there was no need for a transcript of the proceedings if there was no appeal allowed. Records of juvenile proceedings had to be kept sealed anyway, he noted.

JUVENILE JUDGES TAKE A STAND

The state of Arizona won support from two groups of juvenile judges. The Ohio Association of Juvenile Court Judges filed an *amicus* brief supporting Arizona's side in the Gault case, and the Kansas Association of Probate and Juvenile Judges added its name to both the *amicus* brief and the state's brief. The juvenile court's role, the judges said, was to look at why Gerald had misbehaved and find ways to help him. According to the Ohio brief, Gerald was a "full and willing participant" in the incident. His action "might well be taken as presaging much worse trouble to follow." The judges urged the Court to recognize the special needs of children in deciding the case. Unlike adults, children had no right to freedom; they lived under the custody of their parents or, in the case of wayward youngsters, under the state's custody. The brief argued:

> The basic right of a juvenile is not to liberty but to custody. . . . Children are not adults. Their problems, either at home or in the courts, must be met with flexibility and freedom to act in the child's best interests.

Merritt W. Green, who helped draft the brief, argued that "every enlightened government" had the "unquestionable right and imperative duty" to protect and oversee citizens too young or disabled to care for themselves. What troubled youths needed, Green contended, was not adult rights but proper facilities for their care and treatment. Fort Grant, he noted, was a "place of learning" that offered specialized care and treatment for youths. Gerald benefited from commitment to the industrial school, Green said, because his parents were not at home to supervise him and probation had not kept him out of trouble.

Requiring "rigid" procedures in juvenile courts would be a "backward step," Green contended. He claimed that New York's Family Court Act, which required lawyers for juveniles and established more formal procedures, actually hurt juveniles. Under the act, he said, children received treatment only after committing serious offenses. Green conceded that Judge McGhee might have committed procedural errors in Gerald's case. But, he argued, the entire juvenile justice system should not be overhauled because of one judge's error. "It is always easy to second-guess the hard-pressed juvenile court judge," he wrote.

The nine U.S. Supreme Court justices reviewed the detailed arguments in each brief as they worked to reach a decision. According to Court experts, justices rely most heavily on briefs and previous decisions when making a ruling. Rarely does a lawyer win a case based on oral arguments, even if he or she gives a stunning performance. However, lawyers can and do lose cases during orals. In more than one instance, a lawyer's blunder has led to a negative vote. With that in mind, the lawyers in the Gault case prepared their arguments with great care. They would appear before the Court on December 6, 1966.

FIVE
BEFORE THE COURT

NORMAN DORSEN AND HIS WIFE arrived in Washington, D.C., the night before the *Gault* arguments were to take place. He and Daniel Rezneck, his chief adviser, went over every detail of the case, reviewing facts and discussing questions the justice might ask. Dorsen had served as a law clerk for Justice John Marshall Harlan from 1957 to 1958 and was well acquainted with court routine. He knew several of the justices personally.

As he prepared for the next day's presentation, Dorsen felt "fairly certain" that he would have Justices Hugo L. Black, William O. Douglas, William J. Brennan Jr., and possibly Chief Justice Earl Warren on his side. Justice Black, the longest-serving justice, had been a judge and a prosecutor in the lower court system, a lawyer, and a U.S. senator from Alabama before President Franklin D. Roosevelt appointed him to the Court in 1937. He championed constitutional protections, particularly the First Amendment's freedom of speech. Dorsen had encountered the justice many times in his work at the Court.

Justice Douglas, also a Roosevelt appointee, had served on the Court since 1939. A former law professor at Columbia and Yale universities, he fiercely defended individual rights and distrusted government power.

Justice Brennan, whom Dorsen also knew well, frequently voted with Douglas and Black on cases. Appointed to the Court in 1956 by President Dwight D. Eisenhower, Brennan made his mark as a liberal justice whose influence shaped many of the most important cases of the time.

Earl Warren, also an Eisenhower appointee, had served as chief justice since 1953. A skilled leader with liberal views, Warren presided over the Court's consideration of some of the nation's most dramatic and difficult issues, including school desegregation and religion in the schools. The Warren Court had already ruled that adults were entitled to many of the rights now sought by juveniles: the right to counsel, the right against self-incrimination, and other due process issues.

Dorsen was not as confident of the support of the remaining five justices. Justice Harlan, Dorsen's former boss, promoted a strict interpretation of the Constitution. He was less willing than some of his colleagues to stretch the Constitution to cover rights not specifically mentioned in that document. A Rhodes scholar and grandson of the Supreme Court justice for whom he was named, Justice Harlan led the conservative wing of the Court. He was appointed to the Court by Eisenhower in 1955.

Justice Tom C. Clark, appointed by Harry S. Truman, had been on the Court since 1949. A Texas native, he shared his Southern heritage with Justice Black but not Black's passion for the First Amendment. Justice Clark had voted with the majority in the *Gideon* v. *Wainwright* case that guaranteed poor adults the right to free counsel, but he voted against the majority in two later cases (*Escobedo* v. *Illinois* and *Miranda* v. *Arizona*) that protected defendants' right against self-incrimination.

Justice Potter Stewart had served as an appeals court judge before his appointment to the Court in 1958 by Eisenhower. He came from a conservative Republican

THE MEMBERS OF THE U.S. SUPREME COURT, PICTURED IN 1967, WHO HEARD GERALD GAULT'S CASE. SEATED, FROM LEFT: ASSOCIATE JUSTICES JOHN MARSHALL HARLAN AND HUGO L. BLACK, CHIEF JUSTICE EARL WARREN, ASSOCIATE JUSTICES WILLIAM O. DOUGLAS AND WILLIAM J. BRENNAN JR. STANDING, FROM LEFT: ASSOCIATE JUSTICES ABE FORTAS, POTTER STEWART, BYRON R. WHITE, AND THURGOOD MARSHALL.

family, but he often played a centrist role on the Court. As such, he supported both liberal and conservative causes. While siding with Black on most First Amendment cases, Justice Stewart voted against the majority in cases that guaranteed the right to privacy and the right against self-incrimination, as well as a number of other cases he believed went too far in interpreting citizens' constitutional rights.

Justice Byron White, appointed to the Court in 1962 by President John F. Kennedy, was a man who followed widely divergent paths. Before serving on the Court, he played professional football, attended Oxford on a Rhodes

Scholarship, and earned a law degree from Yale. A moderate among liberals on the Warren Court, Justice White had a mixed voting record when it came to constitutional rights. Like Justices Clark and Stewart, he voted for the right to counsel in *Gideon* but against the right to remain silent and other protections in *Escobedo* and *Miranda*.

The newest member on the Court, Justice Abe Fortas had joined the Court in 1965 after being appointed by President Lyndon B. Johnson. A Yale Law School graduate and member of Franklin D. Roosevelt's New Deal, Fortas had argued the *Gideon* case that resulted in a Supreme Court ruling guaranteeing poor defendants the right to counsel. He had served less than a year and a half when the *In re Gault* attorneys presented their case in oral arguments before the Court. In the cases he had participated in, however, Fortas generally voted with the liberal members of the Court. He had written the decision in the *Kent* case that raised grave concerns over the fairness of the juvenile justice system in Washington, D.C.

"EQUAL JUSTICE"

Clouds dulled the sky the morning of December 6, but the weather remained mild for winter. Rezneck and Dorsen went over the case one last time. Dorsen had prepared a written statement of facts, which the two men reviewed together. They walked side by side up the marble steps of the Supreme Court building. The structure is impressive, with its massive marble columns topped by this inscription: "Equal Justice Under Law." More columns greet those who step inside the courtroom where the justices hear the arguments of each case.

As they entered the courtroom, the lawyers on both sides saw the clock hanging from the ceiling, a reminder of the time limit imposed on those who address the Court. In most cases, lawyers are limited to one-half hour to make their case. A yellow light signals that five minutes remain before time is up. When a red light switches on, lawyers must end their argument and sit down. Those who disregard the warnings face a reprimand from the Court and even, on some occasions, an empty bench as impatient justices retreat behind the velvet curtains that separate the courtroom from their chambers.

The nine justices in their black robes sat listening to arguments in another case when Dorsen, his Arizona counterpart, and others connected to the Gault case arrived. Amelia Lewis sat listening to the proceedings. She had paid her own way from Phoenix to hear the arguments in the case she had begun.

STATING GERALD'S CASE

The other case ended, and Gault's lawyers prepared to take their turn. Seated at the left table, directly under the gaze of the justices, the thirty-six-year-old Dorsen felt the tension in the room. Chief Justice Warren, in his reedy voice, called upon Dorsen to begin. "It was my first argument before the Supreme Court," Dorsen later recalled. "I was nervous, but I answered all their questions."

The lawyer began by stating the issue at the heart of the argument. "This case," he told the justices, "raises important Constitutional questions." The Court would be asked to consider whether the Fourteenth Amendment's due process clause, guaranteeing fair treatment, should apply to juveniles. Dorsen promised to address each constitutional safeguard later in his argument: "the right to effective assistance of counsel; the right to adequate notice of the charges of delinquency, including time to prepare; the right to confront and cross-examine the complainant; the privilege against self-incrimination; and the right to a transcript and meaningful judicial review."

As the justices listened, Dorsen outlined the facts of

THE FOURTEENTH AMENDMENT: ENSURING RIGHTS FOR ALL

Section. 1. All persons born or naturalized in the United States and subject to the jurisdiction thereof, are citizens of the United States and of the State wherein they reside. No State shall make or enforce any law which shall abridge the privileges or immunities of citizens of the United States; nor shall any State deprive any person of life, liberty, or property, without due process of law; nor deny to any person within its jurisdiction the equal protection of the laws.

Section. 2. Representatives shall be apportioned among the several States according to their respective numbers, counting the whole number of persons in each State, excluding Indians not taxed. But when the right to vote at any election for the choice of electors for President and Vice President of the United States, Representatives in Congress, the Executive and Judicial officers of a State, or the members of the Legislature thereof, is denied to any of the male inhabitants of such State, being twenty-one years of age, and citizens of the United States, or in any way abridged, except for participation in rebellion, or other crime, the basis of representation therein shall be reduced in the proportion which the number of such male citizens shall bear to the whole number of male citizens twenty-one years of age in such State.

Section. 3. No person shall be a Senator or Representative in Congress, or elector of President and Vice President, or hold any office, civil or military, under the United States, or under any State, who, having previously taken an oath, as a member of Congress, or as an officer of the United States, or as a member of any State legislature, or as an executive or judicial officer of any State, to support the Constitution of the United States, shall have engaged in insurrection or rebellion against the same, or given aid or comfort to the enemies thereof. But Congress may by a vote of two-thirds of each House, remove such disability.

Section. 4. The validity of the public debt of the United States, authorized by law, including debts incurred for payment of pensions and bounties for services in suppressing insurrection or rebellion, shall not be questioned. But neither the United States nor any State shall assume or pay any debt or obligation incurred in aid of insurrection or rebellion against the United States, or any claim for the loss or emancipation of any slave; but all such debts, obligations and claims shall be held illegal and void.

Section. 5. The Congress shall have power to enforce, by appropriate legislation, the provisions of this article.

The First Amendment bars the U.S. Congress from making any law that would establish a particular religion or prevent Americans from freely exercising their religion. It says nothing about what state legislatures can and cannot do.

For years the states used that loophole to pass laws that conflicted with First Amendment protections. In the 1845 case *Permoli* v. *Municipality No. 1 of City of New Orleans*, for example, the Supreme Court upheld Louisiana's argument that the First Amendment did not apply to them. Justice John Catron, writing for the majority, ruled: "The

Constitution makes no provision for protecting the citizens of the respective states in their religious liberties; this is left to the state constitutions and laws."

After the Civil War, Congress sought to close that particular loophole with the passage of the Fourteenth Amendment. Whites in the South had used the loophole to deprive freed slaves of their rights as citizens. With the ratification of the amendment on July 28, 1868, former slaves and all others "born or naturalized in the United States" automatically became American citizens. As citizens, they could vote, own property, and engage in business.

The amendment also directed the states not to deprive anyone, citizen and noncitizen alike, of "life, liberty, or property, without due process of law"; nor the "equal protection of the laws." In addition, the amendment specifically forbade the states from limiting citizens' "privileges or immunities."

For decades after the amendment was passed, however, it offered little protection against state actions. The *Slaughterhouse Cases* set the stage for a conservative view of the amendment.

In March 1869 the Louisiana Legislature granted exclusive rights to the Crescent City Live-Stock Landing and Slaughter-House Company to run slaughterhouses in part of the state. Other slaughterhouse companies objected and filed suit. The U.S. Supreme Court heard the arguments in the suits—which became known as the *Slaughterhouse Cases*—in 1872 and 1873. The plaintiffs argued that the state had deprived them of their rights as citizens to earn a living, guaranteed under the Fourteenth Amendment. They also claimed the Louisiana law denied them "equal protection of the laws" and deprived them of liberty and property "without due process of law," in violation of the Fourteenth Amendment.

The Court ruled against the plaintiffs. In its April 14, 1873, decision, the Court decreed that the Fourteenth Amendment applied only to national rights. The amendment's protections did not extend to state contracts, state elections, or other matters overseen by the state, according to the Court. The ruling allowed states to control the civil rights of their citizens.

Over time, however, the Court began to apply the Fourteenth Amendment to protect citizens against wrongful actions by the states. Under this doctrine, the rights listed in the Bill of Rights are said to be *incorporated* by the Fourteenth Amendment. This doctrine has been referred to as "the second Bill of Rights" because it protected against unreasonable state power as the original ten amendments protected against federal abuses.

The Warren Court in the 1950s and 1960s made extensive use of the incorporation doctrine. With its focus on civil and individual rights, the Warren Court used the doctrine to order school desegregation, ban school prayers, and establish protections for criminal defendants, including juveniles. Later Courts have used the doctrine to strike down state laws banning abortion, to guarantee privacy rights, and to ensure other rights not specifically mentioned in the Constitution.

the case. He told of Ora Cook's complaint about a lewd telephone call, of the boys' being taken into custody, and of officer Flagg's interrogation of Gerald. Dorsen explained that the officers had left no word of Gerald's detention and no notice of the charges against him. The justices heard about Marjorie Gault's trip to the detention home and about the proceedings the following day at which a petition was filed charging Gerald with being a delinquent minor. Dorsen emphasized the point that the petition and related court documents on Gerald were not shown to Marjorie Gault, Gerald, or anyone else in the family until August 17 at the habeas corpus hearing.

The lawyer noted that the court kept no transcript of the proceedings, no one was sworn in, and the court did not advise Gerald or Marjorie Gault of the right to counsel. The lack of a transcript became an issue because the people involved had different recollections of what was said at the proceeding. Marjorie Gault recalled that Gerald told Judge McGhee that his friend Ron Lewis had made the lewd remarks. McGhee and officer Flagg testified that Gerald had admitted saying some of the lewd words. Recollections about the testimony during the second hearing also varied, Dorsen told the Court. Paul and Marjorie Gault recalled that Gerald had admitted nothing. The judge, on the other hand, said Gerald had admitted to making at least some of the remarks. This time, though, officer Flagg agreed with the Gaults' version of the testimony.

Dorsen concluded his rundown of the events leading to the appeal. He told the justices that Marjorie Gault had asked McGhee to call Cook as a witness to identify the caller's voice. The judge refused, saying, "She didn't have to be present." Subsequently, Dorsen said, the judge found that Gerald was a delinquent minor and committed him to the state's industrial school until he reached twenty-one.

In answer to a justice's question, Dorsen noted that

Gerald was fifteen at the time. Justice Fortas, who would conduct most of the questioning during the oral arguments, asked what penalty an adult who committed the same crime would face.

"Two months is the maximum penalty plus a fine," Dorsen replied.

"And this boy got . . . ?" Justice Fortas asked.

"Up to six years," replied Dorsen.

The justices followed with several questions about Fort Grant. Dorsen noted that Gerald lived at the school "under exclusive control" of authorities there. "He can't go home, that's pretty clear," the lawyer replied, confirming a comment by Justice Fortas.

From their questions, Dorsen knew the justices had sympathy for his client. "The justices were very horrified that [Gerald] could be put away for six years for one allegedly dirty phone call when an adult would get two months in jail and all the due process protections," Dorsen recalled later. Justice Fortas, in particular, added weight to Dorsen's points with his well-chosen questions.

Next, Justice Fortas turned to the reasons behind the judge's decision to have Gerald committed. "Did he [Gerald] have any record, other than this purse incident [leading to probation]?" the justice asked Dorsen. The lawyer related the incident in which Gerald was suspected, but never charged, with stealing a baseball glove. "There was no hearing on this, and the case was dropped because there was no material foundation to the claim," Dorsen told the justices. He noted that Judge McGhee had considered Gerald delinquent because he was "habitually involved in immoral matters."

The judge had come to this conclusion apparently based on the boy's probation, the lewd phone call, and the alleged theft of the baseball glove, Dorsen said. The judge had testified at the habeas corpus hearing that he based his ruling on "probably another ground, too," but he did not specify what that might be, Dorsen told the justices. At the same hearing, Dorsen said, the judge testified that he had made his decision based on Gerald's testimony. Dorsen quoted Judge McGhee's statement: "It was all in my mind, done upon the admissions of Gerald Gault." Dorsen noted that "at no point was Gerald informed of a right to remain silent."

Responding to further questions by the justices, Dorsen said the Arizona Supreme Court dismissed the constitutional issues raised in Gerald's appeal. According to Dorsen, the court ruled that Marjorie Gault had sufficient notice of the hearing and charges against Gerald, that "due process does not require that an infant [juvenile] have a right to counsel," and that the Gaults knew they had the option of hiring an attorney. "The court also said that the parents and the probation officer may be relied upon to protect the infant's interests," Dorsen noted. In addition, Dorsen said, the court ruled that cross-examination of witnesses was not required because Gerald had admitted to the charges.

The Arizona court also held that juvenile proceedings would be more likely to achieve "the necessary flexibility for individualized treatment" if youths were not advised of their right to remain silent. Finally, Dorsen told the justices, the lower court had ruled that juveniles had no right of appeal and no right to a transcript.

DEPRIVED OF LIBERTY

Dorsen concluded, "It is [our] position . . . that Gerald Gault was deprived of his liberty without due process of law in the juvenile court of Gila County and that the judgment of the court below should be reversed."

The lawyer interrupted his arguments to give the justices a brief history of the juvenile court system. "The [juvenile] court is theoretically engaged in determining the needs of the child in our society rather than adjudicating guilt and meting out punishment," Dorsen said. "The court and the state are acting as parens patriae rather than prosecutor or judge, treating the child with a firm but benevolent hand." But, he noted, such a system has "led to proceedings in juvenile courts at the expense of certain traditional rights. In some states, courts have ruled that juveniles are not entitled to bail, to indictment, to speedy and public trial, to confrontation of accusers, to the privilege against self-incrimination, and the right to counsel." These rulings, however, drove scholars to reexamine the system and question whether the juvenile court was meeting the goals set when it was originally adopted. And the rulings led them to question "the barter of alleged special treatment for constitutional protection," Dorsen said.

In making his point, he quoted Fortas's decision in the *Kent* case:

> While there can be no doubt of the original laudable purpose of juvenile courts, studies and critiques in recent years raise serious questions as to whether actual performance measures well enough against theoretical purpose to make tolerable the immunity of the process from the reach of constitutional guaranties applicable to adults. There is evidence, in fact, that there may be grounds for concern that the child receives the worst of both worlds: that he gets neither the protections accorded to adults nor the solicitous care and regenerative treatment postulated for children.

Justice Douglas pointed out that the Court, in the *Kent* decision, had not ruled on the constitutional issues cited by Dorsen.

"That's correct," Dorsen replied. But, he added, the Gault case presented the Court with those issues: "whether constitutional guarantees that are applicable to adults must be applied in juvenile court proceedings."

The justices asked whether individual states provided constitutional safeguards to juveniles. Dorsen noted that New York's Family Court Act provided for legal aides to be appointed to represent children's interests. Other areas, too, supplied legal assistance for children, Dorsen said. He based his answer on figures provided in the National Legal Aid and Defender Association brief. He noted that New York and other areas also required that a record be kept of juvenile proceedings.

Justice Fortas posed a question at the heart of the matter. What, he asked, was the "basis for reading the Constitution of the United States so as to carve out juveniles?" Had Dorsen seen the reasons for that?

Dorsen said proponents of the system justified the loss of constitutional safeguards by arguing that they interfered with treatment programs. Such rationalizations, however, were "insufficient," Dorsen said. "We're not saying anything about what treatment a juvenile should receive once they are determined delinquents."

Fortas followed up with another question: Why allow an eighteen-year-old boy to be deprived of constitutional guarantees when such treatment would not be allowed for an adult?

"I see no satisfactory explanation," Dorsen replied.

Justice Brennan offered an answer from the Ohio judges' brief. "What about this theory . . . that fundamentally, the basic right of a juvenile is not for liberty but custody?" The brief, Brennan noted, claimed that "the basic right of a child is custody, whether he's a juvenile delinquent or not; the children of all of us are supposed to be in custody of the parents."

Dorsen rejected the theory but agreed that his opponents used that argument to justify their position. One of the justices noted that setting up an alternative system for juveniles avoided putting an eight-year-old boy on trial, convicting him, and hanging him.

At that point, Chief Justice Warren called a recess for lunch. When Court resumed, Dorsen disputed his opponents' contention that constitutional safeguards would interfere with treatment or undermine the state's custodial obligations toward troubled youths. He noted that both the New Jersey Supreme Court and New York's Family Court Act required the essentials of due process and a fair hearing for juveniles. New York, he added, had two separate hearings for youths: one to determine delinquency and a second to set up a treatment plan or placement in an institution.

Under questioning by the justices, Dorsen described the New York act in more detail. It provided counsel for children, granted the right against self-incrimination, and required that the facts of the case be given to the child in writing. Hearings remained closed without a jury trial, but the New York law provided for appeals and transcripts of proceedings. Witnesses could be cross-examined, and the court could not rely solely on a juvenile's confession to prove the case against the youth.

WHAT IS LEFT OF THE SYSTEM?

If youths were guaranteed all those constitutional rights, Justice Tom C. Clark wondered, "what is left of the juvenile system?"

"The best part," Dorsen quickly replied. The attorney said later that he was proudest of that response. Once a child had "properly been determined to be a juvenile [delinquent]," Dorsen told the Court, the state would have the opportunity "to treat him, to take care of him, to rehabilitate him." He pointed out that under the current system, three-fourths of the states allowed juveniles to be placed in prisons with adult criminals.

Later in the arguments, Dorsen said he might approve of a system where welfare workers or other staff not involved in the delinquency hearing could talk confidentially with the boy without a lawyer present. "But that would be a very specially constructed system," Dorsen noted, "and I would have to see it before I would want to [approve it]."

Justice Brennan raised the question of public trials for youths. A public trial—or a trial by jury—was one of the few rights Dorsen did not pursue for his young client. He noted that a child should not have to undergo a public trial because of a "special sensitivity to publicity, the special stigma that might attach to the child, and the child's disorientation before the public." Even with a closed trial and sealed records, however, proceedings were far from confidential. Dorsen acknowledged, in response to a question by Justice Fortas, that draft authorities, the FBI, and local police all had access to juvenile records.

Justice Black questioned how one could distinguish between a boy of nineteen and a man of twenty-three when considering whether to have a public trial. "If you stick to words in the Constitution and forget the words 'fundamental fairness,' what would you do?"

"That would present a hard question," Dorsen replied. His answer drew the laughter of the justices.

Dorsen devoted the rest of his time to discussing how the lack of constitutional safeguards harmed young Gerald. "[T]his boy was prejudiced against in countless ways not only because of the absence of counsel but because at no time was either he or his parents informed of the specific charge upon which the judge ultimately made a decision. If a lawyer were present, for example, the lawyer would have tried to establish exactly what the charge was."

Once again, Justice Fortas underscored Dorsen's point with his own comments. "As a matter of fact, I'm still not clear [on what the charge was]. . . All we have here are these vague remarks [by the judge]."

Another justice (not identified on the transcript) offered an explanation. "The determination of delinquency depends not on specific acts of misconduct but on . . . the totality of his [Gerald's] previous conduct." In that way, the juvenile proceeding differed from an adult trial where only the specific crime under investigation could be discussed in court. Dorsen, however, noted that even with that difference, juveniles should still be given the opportunity to dispute the facts presented.

Justice Fortas added his thoughts: "The theory is that there are specific incidents upon which a finding of delinquency has to be made. Not some general amorphous reaction to the boy." In Gerald's case, he noted, the evidence was thin. "There's nothing in this record that illuminates what that baseball glove incident was, nothing beyond the bare words of the report with respect to the purse taking."

The justices questioned the extent of constitutional protections in other states' juvenile courts. Dorsen cited the Legal Aid brief in noting that many states provided juveniles a right to counsel, a right to remain silent, a right to appeal, and a right to confront witnesses. "In other words," he said, "it has come to be recognized over the past few years . . . that these rights are essential; that they are in no way inconsistent with the therapeutic and dispositional aspects of the juvenile proceeding; that the specific facts, as Mr. Justice Fortas stated, are those that have to be rebutted; that [having] a lawyer is as essential or more essential in juvenile cases than it is with adults."

Dorsen noted that 74 percent of the states provided attorneys to children who could not afford to hire their own. He disputed the Arizona Supreme Court's premise that a parent or the probation officer could act on behalf of the child in place of a lawyer. "If the parent himself were before the court as a defendant," Dorsen argued, "he would be entitled to a lawyer on the theory that he couldn't defend his own case. But when the child is in the position of defendant, when the child is before the court with up to six years of his freedom to be lost, somehow the Arizona Supreme Court finds that the parent can satisfactorily act on behalf of the child as a lawyer would."

Proposing that a probation officer could serve as a child's advocate was even more far-fetched, Dorsen said. "There's a flat-out conflict of interest. . . . [Probation officer] Flagg did not do a thing for Gerald Gault. It is well established that he did not inform Gerald Gault of any of his rights throughout the proceeding. Instead what he did try to do was to get a change of story. . . . He was certainly acting as an adversary."

Dorsen noted that not allowing attorneys did not ensure that the proceedings would be harmonious and nonadversarial. "Instead," he said, "it means that we'll have a one-sided adversarial proceeding, in which the cards are stacked against the child from beginning to end."

In answer to Justice White's queries, Dorsen said the child should receive a notice of charges and a hearing in writing. "It's his interests that are at stake." He added that parents, too, should be notified.

"Why to the parent," White asked. "If someone brings a charge against me, they don't notify my mother, do they?"

Dorsen replied that parents were "in a position to help the child." All jurisdictions polled by the legal aid office notified parents, he said. With just a few minutes remaining, Dorsen postponed the rest of his remarks until after Arizona's lawyer had presented his case.

Arizona Makes Its Case

Frank A. Parks began forcefully. "The attack that is being made today against the Arizona juvenile code goes in our estimation to the heart of the American juvenile court system," he told the justices. "We the appellees in this case consider this the crossroads of juvenile jurisprudence." For two-thirds of a century, Parks said, the juvenile court system had weathered constitutional attacks. Everyone in the case agreed, he noted, that children needed to be treated differently from adults. The conflict, he said, arose from the requirements of due process on the one hand and the "sociologist's concept" of the best treatment for a troubled child.

Justice White asked whether the case's outcome would be a crossroads for juvenile courts in other states like New York or California. New York had already gone beyond that point, Parks said, and California had "made an inroad on their crossroad." That brought laughter from the bench.

Justice White made the point, and Parks agreed, that only certain states, including Arizona, might be dramatically affected by the case. The questioning switched to Justice Fortas, who wanted to know which constitutional safeguards Parks believed would interfere with treatment of juveniles. Would providing a written notice to the child and the parent disrupt treatment? Allowing an appeal?

No, Parks replied, neither safeguard would interfere with treatment.

Cross-examining a witness? Fortas asked.

Parks had mixed feelings about that issue. Cross-examining a witness, he said, might be required for a fair trial if the youth did not admit guilt. If the juvenile did admit wrongdoing, as Gerald had, confronting witnesses would be unnecessary. "The one potential disadvantage to confrontation," he told the Court, "is to bring the child into the center of an adversarial proceeding with all the taint perhaps of a criminal proceeding that we try to remove from the child." Cross-examining witnesses might not be necessary even if the child denied guilt, Park said. "It would be incumbent upon the discretionary powers of the judge to ensure that the subject is aired . . . to his satisfaction and by clear and convincing evidence [to] indicate that there has been a violation, if there is a violation, or that the facts alleged indeed did take place."

"Do you know any way of establishing anything by clear and convincing evidence short of providing fundamental due process?" Fortas pressed.

"The two go hand in hand, your honor," Parks responded. That said, however, he argued that telling a child he could remain silent or appointing a lawyer for him or her would "definitely" interfere with treatment. "It is the state's last opportunity to take a child of tender years and in a very, very supreme effort to try to take that child, who is perhaps incorrigible, and make him a good citizen," Parks told the Court. "Now to tell him at the outset we're here for your benefit, anything you say may be used against you, you don't have to say anything. . . . I think that even the experts will indicate this is a very, very bad first step."

Parks estimated that only about 20 percent of the youth placed at Fort Grant returned to serve time for later misdeeds.

CHILDREN DIFFERENT FROM ADULTS

He asked the Court to keep in mind that children were different from adults. "All through a child's adolescent years, he goes through a period of limited freedom. He doesn't know absolute liberty and freedom such is known to an adult. He has no absolute right to go out and drive a car; he has a limited right to contract; he doesn't have the personal liberty to avoid compulsory education. His entire adolescent years, in many cases a direct indication of just how he is going to be brought up, is directly dependent on what proper parental restraints are placed upon on him." The juvenile court, Parks noted, had to step in to oversee a child's custody, and apply the necessary restraints, when a parent could not, or would not, fill that role.

For the most part, Parks agreed with Dorsen's rendition of events. But he emphasized that probation officer Flagg "explained everything" to Marjorie Gault when she came looking for Gerald at the detention center. Parks also contended that Gerald told the judge he had made some of the lewd calls. "We don't think it was a case where the child denied [the deed]."

Justice Fortas questioned the good intentions of the state in Gerald's case. "So this supposedly benevolent parens patria, the state, picks the boy up and puts him in what in most jurisdictions one would have to say is whimsically called a receiving home." The justice's tone as well as his words revealed his doubts. But Parks met the challenge. With good humor he replied, "We like to think [of] detention centers as getting the center of our attention, Mr. Justice Fortas." Justice Fortas remained unconvinced, however. "Then I'd say you're relatively unique."

Chief Justice Warren interrupted the volley with a question of his own. Was anyone in the household, he asked, notified where the boy had gone? Parks tried to justify the lack of notice. Officer Flagg, he said, had been out of his office for the day and met Marjorie Gault at the detention center soon after he returned. "We would presume that if he had been there earlier, there would have been an actual notice," Parks told the chief justice. He noted that Gerald and his family were not "new to this type of state action," since Gerald had been in trouble before.

That raised the issue of the baseball glove. Parks noted that in a small office like Flagg's, the probation officers and the judge would be well aware of the facts of the case even if it did not go to court and there was no record of it. "The judge was there back in 1962. His probation officers were there in 1962, and they handled it," Parks said.

That did not appease Justice Fortas, however. "I have no way of knowing if that's so or that it's not so," he told Parks. "The fact of the matter is, based on what you say and what happened here, is that was an important reason, an unwritten, unknown, and perhaps so far as we know an unadmitted, unproven incident [that] was part of the reason for putting the boy in detention for a maximum of six years."

Parks admitted that was so. But he pointed out that the judge relied on other factors as well, including Gerald's probation and the fact that he was not responding to the treatment already ordered by the court. Justice Fortas, however, found little substance in the other charges. "So far as this record shows on that grand theft incident," he told Parks, "the only thing we have, a scrap of paper that is reproduced in this record, that shows he was in the theater along with another boy and that the other boy took the pocketbook. . . . We don't know whether the boy himself was culpable, what the degree of culpability was, whether he participated in taking it, or whether he was just along with the boy."

Again, Parks was forced to admit that Fortas was correct. He won a temporary reprieve, however, from Justice Black. In response to Justice Black's question, Parks noted that the Arizona juvenile court in its dealings with Gerald had followed procedure common in many jurisdictions. "I don't see you've done anything extraordinarily bad," Black responded.

Parks agreed. "The case law up until now is relatively replete with cases that have passed on these same identical subjects where the courts have accepted the parens patriae doctrine," he said. "They have balanced on the one hand, . . . the needs of the individual and on the other hand, just what the goals of equality are . . . We're trying to equalize what is needed and what is required."

In responding to further questions from Justice Black, Parks found himself in a small hole. He tried to equate conditions at the industrial school with those at home. "We tend to think it's not confinement merely because his liberty is limited to the parental restraint level," he told the justice. But Justice Black did not buy the argument. "He's not confined?" he asked. "Maybe you went a little too far then." While conceding that youths did not have the right to walk away from the industrial school any time they chose, Parks resisted the suggestion that Gerald was imprisoned there. "The child is sent there for training," he said. "It's just like . . . you're going to school from eight until four or whatever the hours are and you may leave at four o'clock and come home."

"Could he?" Justice Black prompted.

Parks had to admit defeat. "Well," he replied, "he is there on a twenty-four-hour basis." Chuckles rose from the bench at that admission.

The discussion shifted to Gerald's parents. Parks noted that Gerald's father was often away from home, and the court did not think the parents provided enough supervision. "If you've got a good child who is not being helped by his parents as he should," Parks said, "the state has an interest in that child to attempt to keep him on the straight road of life until he gets to the age of twenty-one when he's on his own." It was up to the judge, Parks added, to determine if the youngster would benefit from a stay at an industrial school or from stricter rules at home.

In Gerald's case, Parks noted, the punishment was much less severe than originally ordered by the judge. The boy stayed at Fort Grant full-time for only five months. After that, authorities allowed him to go home on weekends and receive training at the industrial school during the week. Park said Gerald now lived with his parents. "[Institute officials] applied what they thought was needed on the boy and now he hasn't been in trouble," Parks told the court. Gerald continued under the jurisdiction of the institution, however. "At any time," Parks said, "he could be taken back without a hearing."

Chief Justice Warren raised the question, again, of cross-examining Ora Cook. "What about that [not requiring her to testify] so far as a fair hearing is concerned?"

Parks repeated his assertion that there was no need to question Ora Cook because Gerald had already admitted the act. The need for cross-examination, he noted, depended on whether, "when in a friendly manner, the juvenile judge said, 'Gerald, what went on, what did you do?' and the boy says, 'Well, judge, I called the number and I said some of the words on the phone.'"

That brought a quick response from Justice Fortas and laughter from the audience: "Suppose the judge didn't say it in a fatherly manner?" Just as quickly, Parks responded: "Then I'd say he wasn't an Arizona juvenile court judge, Mr. Justice Fortas."

Other justices pursued the issue. Why, they wanted to know, did the court not call in Ora Cook after Gerald denied making the lewd comments? Parks repeated his contention that Gerald had admitted his guilt and therefore no witnesses were required. The Arizona Supreme Court, Parks noted, had rejected the Gaults' and officer

CHIEF JUSTICE EARL WARREN

Flagg's statements that Gerald had recanted. Instead the court chose to believe Judge McGhee's report that the boy had admitted the deed.

Fortas again took up the questioning. Did Arizona allow children to be declared delinquent based solely on a youth's confession, without corroborating evidence of misbehavior? He noted that some states required more than a juvenile's confession. Parks did not know of specific cases involving the issue, but said he believed that a youth's confession would be accepted without requiring further evidence.

ATTORNEYS NOT NEEDED
The lawyer moved on to what he considered to be the most important issue in the case, the right to counsel. He began

by arguing that a juvenile proceeding was not a criminal trial. Juveniles found to be delinquent were not convicted of a crime. Arizona protected the child by ordering that all records of the proceedings be destroyed after two years, according to Parks.

Under questioning from Justice Fortas, however, Parks conceded that the law required only that records of the proceedings be destroyed. In Gerald's case, Parks admitted, mention of the boy's committal to the institution and background material might remain in the records.

"Which is cold comfort," Justice Fortas commented. "There still would be a record that the boy was sent to the institution for such and such a period for such and such on such and such a basis."

Parks agreed to the possibility, but continued on with his main point: that lawyers were not necessary because the state was working for the benefit of youths in trouble. "We try to remove as much of a traumatic experience for the child as possible," he said. Probation officers acted on behalf of the child, Parks contended, despite Dorsen's claim to the contrary. He argued strongly against a rule that would require lawyers for children. The juvenile court needed more flexibility, he asserted, noting that judges could and did appoint lawyers when they believed it necessary.

Parents who could afford it had the option of hiring an attorney for their child, Parks said in response to a question by Chief Justice Warren. Poor children, whose parents could not afford an attorney, had to rely on the probation officer or hope that the judge would agree to appoint an attorney for them.

"Do you think it represents fair play for the judge himself to determine whether a child shall have counsel?" Chief Justice Warren asked.

"Yes," Parks replied. The judge would appoint a lawyer "if the circumstances of the case warrant[ed] it."

Parks used his remaining time to explain why he believed children should not be informed of the right against self-incrimination. First, he noted, the child did not face a criminal conviction even if he or she admitted guilt. Second, the court did not punish a child for remaining silent. However, Parks stated, a child's refusal to talk to the judge or officers often "just indicates the fact that the child is antagonistic to society, unwilling to cooperate, showing a need for . . . additional guidance." The judge's role, he said, was to talk "with the child in a most reasonable respect, encouraging him to tell the truth." He also repeated his conviction that due process did not require juvenile proceedings to have transcripts or allow appeals.

SPEAKING FOR THE JUDGES

Parks turned over the few minutes he had left to Merritt W. Green, attorney for the Ohio Association of Juvenile Court Judges. Green said he spoke for "the thousands of people who preside over and work within the framework of the juvenile court system." He expressed concern that a decision in the Gault case "would in effect wipe out our present juvenile court procedure structures." Just as the court system had separate standards for felonies and misdemeanors, Green said, the courts treated children differently from adults.

Justice Fortas took issue with Green's comparison. Felonies were distinct from misdemeanors, he said, because the acts were different. But, he noted, there might be no difference between a felony and delinquency except in the age of the person who committed the act.

Green agreed, but argued that children did not commit crimes; they became delinquent. Only when the juvenile court transferred them to adult court did they stand accused of crimes. And it was only then, he said, that they had need of the constitutional safeguards under discussion.

But Justice Fortas did not accept Green's carefully drawn distinctions. "What is the difference, Mr. Green?" he asked the lawyer.

> If an adult had done exactly the same thing [as Gerald], he would have been arrested, he would have been tried, he would have been given due process, he'd have a right against self-incrimination, he would have the possibility of appeal, there would have been a transcript, there would have been notice in writing, the burden would have been on the state to establish his guilt beyond reasonable doubt, there would have been confrontational witnesses, all because he's an adult. And the most he could have been put away for is two months. Now here's a boy that gets picked up. He gets none of these safeguards. . . . And he gets sent up for a maximum possibility of being deprived of his freedom for six years. Why do you call one a crime and not the other a crime?

Green retreated somewhat. But he continued to maintain that juveniles' behavior was viewed differently from that of adults and therefore the courts granted youngsters special treatment. He noted, too, that the court determined Gerald's delinquency not just on the phone incident but on his past behavior.

Justice Fortas pushed Green to explain why Gerald should not have had "the basic elements of a trial" to determine exactly what the boy had done and how it led to a delinquency ruling. "Now is it your position that knowing that would destroy the juvenile court theory?" he asked.

"Decidedly not," Green quickly replied. He assured the justice that "all courts and all of us here say that due processes certainly should be accorded to juveniles." But he qualified that. Due process, he speculated, might differ from case to case. "I don't think there's a hard and fast rule that due process is this in every case," Green said.

As he had with Parks, Justice Fortas led Green through a laundry list of rights to be required by due process. Green agreed to adequate notice and counsel, but when the justice mentioned self-incrimination, the lawyer balked. "Constitutional protections . . . apply where a person is charged with a crime," he said. If all the constitutional guarantees applied in juvenile cases, he reasoned, then delinquency might as well be considered a crime.

Green's argument did little to persuade Fortas. "I don't get anywhere by trying to solve this problem in terms of the use of a word like crime or not crime," he told the lawyer. "We're dealing with proceedings here in which persons may be deprived of their liberty. They're in custody. You can call it a crime or you can call it a horse, they're still deprived of liberty."

"But children are not adults," Green insisted. "I think we recognize in this society that there are certain restraints that must be on children, and that some children by reason of certain circumstances require restraints, guidance, training over and beyond [what] they get within the natural custody of their family." In answer to a final question by Justice Fortas, Green reiterated the position that cross-examination of witnesses was necessary only when the child did not admit guilt.

Chief Justice Warren asked the lawyer if members of a national association of juvenile judges agreed with his position. To the side, a justice's comment that "they probably can't agree on anything" injected a bit of humor into the proceedings. Pausing to let the laughter subside,

Green said he believed juvenile justices agreed that the system's treatment of juveniles was not at all like proceedings in adult criminal court.

FINAL ARGUMENTS

After Green sat down, Dorsen used the last of his time to make his final points. First, he assailed Judge McGhee's failure to use his discretion to appoint a lawyer for Gerald. "The record is literally teeming with unresolved issues," Dorsen told the Court, "and I can't understand why the discretion wasn't exercised." The judge's inaction highlighted the folly of leaving such discretion in the hands of one person. In making that point, Dorsen quoted a famous passage Justice Douglas had written in his dissent in the 1951 case, *United States* v. *Wunderlich*: "Absolute discretion is a ruthless master. It is more destructive of freedom than any of man's other inventions."

Second, under questioning by Justice White, Dorsen argued that every child should be represented by a lawyer during delinquency hearings. "There would have to be a lawyer in the courtroom every time there is a determination?" White asked, and Dorsen agreed.

His third point focused on Gerald's right to be warned that he did not have to testify against himself. "We believe there is a clear case of possible self-incrimination under the Arizona code," he told the justices. In his final statements, Dorsen reexamined the testimony by the Gaults, Judge McGhee, and officer Flagg on what Gerald said during the hearings. "It doesn't sound to me that Gerald Gault specifically admitted making those statements," Dorsen said.

With the oral arguments at an end, the justices rose and filed out behind the curtains to their chambers. There, shielded from press and public, they would debate the issues and decide the future of the nation's juvenile court.

SIX
THE DECISION

THE NINE JUSTICES of the U.S. Supreme Court set Fridays aside to discuss the cases they have heard during the week. They meet in a private conference room; only the justices themselves attend. The chief justice speaks first. He is followed by the associate justice who has served the longest on the Court. Then the remaining members of the Court, speaking in order of their seniority, comment on the case under discussion.

After everyone has spoken, the justices may vote on the case. The newest members of the Court vote first so that they will not be influenced by the votes of the more experienced justices. The cases are decided by a simple majority.

If the chief justice votes with the majority, he may choose to write the opinion himself. Or he may assign the task to an associate justice on the majority side. In cases where the chief justice is in the minority, the justice with the most seniority who has voted with the majority decides who will write the opinion.

It may take several months for the justices to decide a case. They may vote many times before finally resolving the issues. In particularly important cases—like the school desegregation case—the chief justice may delay a vote in order to win unanimous support.

Once the majority opinion has been written, the justices review it and decide whether to add their names to it. Sometimes justices will change their votes—either for or against—after reading the opinion. If enough justices change their votes, a new majority opinion—this time on the opposite side—has to be written. At times, justices object to the finished version of the opinion and ask that it be rewritten.

Justices who vote with the majority but whose reasons differ from those stated in the Court's decision may write a concurrence. These documents may explore issues not mentioned in the majority opinion or they may emphasize certain points. Those who disagree with the Court's decision may write a dissent stating their reasons for opposing the vote. A justice may "join" a colleague's concurrence or dissent by adding his or her name to the opinion. Some of the Court's most famous statements have appeared in dissents. Later Courts may adopt the dissenting views and overturn the original decision.

Concurrences and dissents do not become part of the law and do not affect the decision. They may, however, influence public opinion. A decision often carries more weight with the public if all nine justices stand behind it. Nevertheless, a decision supported by a one-vote margin stands as law on the same footing as a unanimous decision. Lower courts are obligated to follow its dictates.

Landmark Decision

Five months after hearing oral arguments, the Supreme Court announced its decision in the Gault case. On May 15, 1967, Justice Abe Fortas read the decision he had written for the Court. By an 8 to 1 vote, the Court overturned the actions of the Arizona courts and ruled in favor of Gerald Gault. The landmark decision gave juveniles throughout the country many of the rights guaranteed to

ASSOCIATE JUSTICE ABE FORTAS WROTE THE MAJORITY OPINION IN *IN RE GAULT* THAT GAVE JUVENILES MANY OF THE RIGHTS OF ADULT DEFENDANTS.

adult defendants by the Constitution. Previous cases had already "unmistakably indicate[d]" that "neither the Fourteenth Amendment nor the Bill of Rights is for adults alone," Fortas said.

"Under our Constitution, the condition of being a boy does not justify a kangaroo court," the justice wrote in his hard-hitting opinion. In cases such as Gerald's, Fortas noted, juveniles faced confinement for a long period of time. "In view of this, it would be extraordinary if our Constitution did not require the procedural regularity and the exercise of care implied in the phrase 'due process.'"

The Court decision extended to juveniles most of the Constitutional safeguards sought by Gault:

Adequate notice of charges. According to the ruling, the Gaults were not given adequate notice, despite the state of Arizona's claim that Mrs. Gault "knew the exact nature of the charge" against Gerald. To meet the Constitution's requirements, suspects must be given written notice of specific charges, and they must be given enough time to prepare a case. Due process, Fortas said, "does not allow a hearing to be held in which a youth's freedom and his parents' right to his custody are at stake without giving them timely notice, in advance of the hearing, of the specific issues that they must meet."

The right to counsel. A child facing confinement in a state institution needs an attorney's help "to cope with problems of law, to make skilled inquiry into the facts, to insist upon regularity of the proceedings, and to ascertain whether he has a defense and to prepare and submit it," Justice Fortas wrote in the opinion. "The child 'requires the guiding hand of counsel at every step in the proceedings against him,'" he added, quoting from an earlier decision.

Many juvenile justice groups, municipalities, and child welfare organizations shared that view, he said. Among them, the justice cited the President's Crime

Commission; the Children's Bureau of the United States Department of Health, Education, and Welfare; and the National Council of Juvenile Court Judges. He noted that the New York Family Court Act, in its regulations, included the right of counsel for juveniles. With the *In re Gault* ruling, the Supreme Court guaranteed the right to counsel for youths in all future delinquency hearings:

> We conclude that the Due Process Clause of the Fourteenth Amendment requires that in respect of proceedings to determine delinquency which may result in commitment to an institution in which the juvenile's freedom is curtailed, the child and his parents must be notified of the child's right to be represented by counsel retained by them, or if they are unable to afford counsel, that counsel will be appointed to represent the child.

The right to remain silent. Children have as much right as anyone else not to incriminate themselves, the Court ruled. And they in particular need to be told that they do not have to say anything that could be used against them. "It would indeed be surprising if the privilege against self-incrimination were available to hardened criminals but not to children," Justice Fortas wrote. One reason this right is so important, he said, is to ensure that confessions, when they are made, are the truth and not the result of fear or coercion. He noted that the New York Family Court Act required police and the court to contact the parents, if possible, before questioning juveniles. It also required that both parents and children be told at the start of a hearing that the child had a right to remain silent. Justice Fortas cited several cases where children under pressure from police grilling had "confessed" to crimes they did not commit.

The opinion discounted the argument that youths do not need a safeguard against self-incrimination because juvenile proceedings are civil, not criminal. First, Fortas noted, a ruling of delinquency can result in the loss of freedom for a youngster. In some states, he noted, juveniles may even end up in adult jails as a result of such a ruling. Commitment—whether to an institution or to a jail and whether it is called a civil or a criminal proceeding—is still "a deprivation of liberty," Fortas wrote. "And our Constitution guarantees that no person shall be 'compelled' to be a witness against himself when he is threatened with deprivation of his liberty."

Secondly, Fortas said, the juvenile court has the authority to transfer a child's case to adult court, where everything the child has said can and will be used against him or her.

Fortas also dismissed the state's claims that warning children of their right to remain silent would make them hostile and less willing to cooperate with authorities in setting up an appropriate treatment plan. The justice maintained that often the opposite was true. Forcing children to answer questions does not aid in "individualized treatment," nor does it serve "any other good purpose," according to the opinion. Instead, children who have been forced to answer questions and are then disciplined as a result of their statements are likely to be hostile. "The child may well feel that he has been led or tricked into confession and despite his confession, he is being punished," Fortas wrote.

Further, Fortas noted, statements by youngsters are often untrustworthy. The courts, he said, must ensure that children's admissions are not "the product of ignorance of rights or of adolescent fantasy, fright, or despair."

The right to cross-examine witnesses. Justice Fortas rejected Arizona's contention that Gerald had no right to confront Ora Cook in court because he had already admitted guilt. Since Gerald lacked safeguards against self-incrimination, any statements he made should be disregarded, according to the justice. Without a valid confession, Fortas said, it was "essential" that witnesses be sworn in, allowed to testify, and be available for cross-examination. Lacking such testimony, the juvenile court could not justify a finding of delinquency and an order that could have resulted in Gerald's being confined for six years. The opinion quoted the *Kent* decision to make the point: "There is no place in our system of law for reaching a result of such tremendous consequences without ceremony."

The decision did not address the issue of right of appeal or right of a transcript. Fortas noted, however, that the juvenile court's failure to allow an appeal, to provide a transcript, and to give the reasons behind the judge's decision in Gerald's case left the reviewing court "with the burden of attempting to reconstruct a record," and imposed on the judge "the unseemly duty of testifying under cross-examination as to the events that transpired in the hearings."

INDISPENSABLE FOUNDATION OF INDIVIDUAL FREEDOM

In his opinion, Fortas stressed the importance of due process in ensuring fair treatment under law. He noted, "Due process of law is the primary and indispensable foundation of individual freedom." It "defines the rights of the individual" and sets limits on the state's power over individual people. Procedural rules help courts uncover the truth amid "opposing versions and conflicting data."

The state claimed that the special procedures in juvenile courts offset the loss of due process and made it unnecessary. Such claims, Fortas said, should not go unchallenged. He cited reports that showed juvenile crime had increased and juvenile offenders had returned to court repeatedly, despite the system's special procedures.

Fortas took care to note that the Court required constitutional safeguards only during proceedings to determine a youth's guilt or that could result in loss of liberty or other penalty. The Court order did not apply to proceedings where staff worked with troubled youth to develop treatment plans. Those sessions were "unique to the juvenile process," Fortas said, and since they did not involve a penalty, the safeguards did not apply. The ruling did not address whether due process had to be followed at hearings to determine what should be done with youths who were judged to be delinquents.

The claim that the juvenile court protected youths by keeping proceedings confidential, Fortas said, was "more rhetoric than reality." Judges, he said, could decide when to keep records closed and when to open them to view. Many jurisdictions destroyed only the record of hearings; other records remained intact. In addition, most courts turned records over to the police, the FBI, and the military, and in some cases, potential employers. In any case, Fortas noted, providing constitutional safeguards would not undermine the confidentiality of the proceedings.

Justice Fortas also rejected the state's claim that juvenile facilities were schools rather than prisons. The justice's description of life at a state institution revealed the hard, cold reality of what Gerald Gault had endured:

> A boy is charged with misconduct. The boy is committed to an institution where he may be restrained of liberty for years. . . . His world becomes "a building with whitewashed walls, regimented routine and institutional hours . . . ."

Instead of mother and father and sisters and brothers and friends and classmates, his world is peopled by guards, custodians, state employees, and "delinquents" confined with him for anything from waywardness to rape and homicide.

Youths deserved a careful inquiry and "the essentials of due process" before being consigned to such a fate, Fortas declared. If Gerald had been an adult, the justice wrote, he would have been entitled to all the rights and protections available under the Constitution: the right to counsel, the right to notice, and all the other rights afforded in a criminal court. As it did in the *Kent* case, the Court held that, under the Constitution, youths as well as adults had a right to fair treatment.

Due process requirements did not prevent juvenile courts from treating juveniles differently from adults, nor did they eliminate the juvenile court's benefits, Fortas noted. Under the ruling, juveniles would still be tried and treated separately from adult offenders. They would continue to avoid criminal labels, and their records would be kept private. The new rules, Fortas noted, would not prevent a "kindly juvenile judge" from continuing to act out of concern for the young offender in court.

Without due process safeguards, however, Gerald Gault faced punishment far greater than an adult would have endured. In fact, the justice noted, not only did the Arizona juvenile court deprive Gerald Gault of a fair hearing; it also failed to meet the original goals of the juvenile court system. Those goals, Fortas said, required that the court take the time and use care to find out exactly what the youngster had done and what had led to his or her actions. "Was it a prank of adolescence or a brutal act threatening serious consequences to himself or society unless corrected?" the justice asked. In Gerald's case,

Fortas noted, "one would assume . . . where the juvenile appears to have a home, a working mother and father, and an older brother, the Juvenile Judge would have made a careful inquiry and judgment as to the possibility that the boy could be disciplined and dealt with at home, despite his previous transgressions."

That, of course, did not happen. The main difference between Gerald's case and an adult offender's case was the lack of any safeguards to protect Gerald's rights, Fortas said. "So wide a gulf between the State's treatment of the adult and of the child," Fortas wrote, required "a bridge sturdier" than mere words.

MIDDLE GROUND

Despite the Court's firm support of due process for juveniles, it stopped short of ordering for juveniles all the rights available to adults. Under the ruling, juveniles whose cases were considered by a juvenile court could not be indicted by a grand jury and had no right to public trial by jury. In writing the *In re Gault* decision, Justice Abe Fortas negotiated between two extremes:

> 1) leaving the juvenile courts as they were and thus abandoning youths to the arbitrary power of juvenile judges, or
> 2) eliminating the juvenile court system altogether and treating juvenile cases in the same way as those of adults.

Justice Fortas and the Court sought a middle ground. By granting juveniles some (but not all) of the rights accorded adults, the Court provided youngsters protection from judges who abused their power. But Fortas made it clear that juvenile proceedings were not to be the same as adult trials. Under the ruling, juveniles must be treated

fairly as required by the due process clause of the
Fourteenth Amendment. However, unlike adults, children
could not claim all the safeguards (including trial by jury
and public trials) provided by the Bill of Rights. Fortas
hoped that by limiting youths' rights in that way, juvenile
courts would retain the flexibility needed to work effec-
tively with troubled youths. As long as the juvenile court
treated its young charges fairly (and saw to it that the four
specified rights were protected), the juvenile court could
continue to operate apart from the adult criminal system.

concurrences

Four justices wrote separate opinions in the case. Three
concurred with the majority opinion; one dissented.
Justice Hugo Black voted with the majority, but he was the
only one who believed that the Bill of Rights protected
children and adults equally. But even Fortas's handling of
the issue, he said, would strike "a well-nigh fatal blow to
much that is unique about the juvenile courts in the
Nation." He noted that from the beginning the juvenile
court had failed to meet its goal of saving young offenders
from "youthful indiscretions and stigmas." That failure
was evident in the Gault case. Instead of fulfilling its goal
to "lighten or avoid punishment for criminality," the
Arizona juvenile court system ordered Gerald to six years
of confinement "in what is in all but name a penitentiary
or jail," according to Black. In such cases where children
lose their freedom, the justice said, "it would be a plain
denial of equal protection of the laws—an invidious dis-
crimination" to deny the offenders the same constitutional safeguards available to adults.

Black agreed with Fortas that Gerald and his parents
were entitled to the rights outlined in the opinion. But he
took issue with the notion that the Court should determine which rights should apply to juvenile courts. Black

JUSTICES SPEAK THEIR MINDS: HOW SEPARATE OPINIONS INFLUENCE LAW

The U.S. Supreme Court is the highest court in the land. Its decisions are final. A Supreme Court decision can be overturned only by another decision issued by a later Court or by a constitutional amendment. Among the most notable decisions later invalidated was the *Dred Scott* ruling, in which the Court determined that blacks were not citizens and were not entitled to protection by the federal government. The decision was overturned by the Thirteenth and Fourteenth Amendments, which abolished slavery and established that everyone born in the United States was automatically a citizen with equal rights.

Usually the Court bases its decisions on precedent, rulings that previous Courts have made. Only in extreme circumstances does the Court reverse an earlier decision.

The majority opinion—the ruling agreed to by five or more justices—establishes the law in the matter. A ruling requires only a simple majority—five of the nine justices on a full Court. The justices, appointed for life, each have an equal vote. Usually the chief justice, if he agrees with the majority, either writes the majority decision himself or appoints an associate justice also on the winning side to take on the task. When the chief justice is on the losing side, the most-senior associate justice who has voted with the majority makes the assignment.

Justices can write their own opinions on any case they wish. If they agree with the majority vote but have different reasons for their views, or want to comment on the case further, they can submit a concurrence. Those who disagree with a majority opinion can submit a dissent. Sometimes a justice writes a separate opinion so well that other justices are persuaded to join the dissent or concurrence. Occasionally enough justices decide to join a separate opinion that it becomes the majority opinion. At times, the vote has shifted sides when justices withdrew from the majority decision to join a dissent.

Justice Tom Clark once said, "You know, we don't have money at the Court for an army, and we can't take ads in the newspapers, and we don't want to go out on a picket line in our robes. We have to convince the nation by the force of our opinions." That force can be—and occasionally is—undermined by opposing justices' separate opinions in a case. If a case is particularly controversial, a justice's separate opinion—sometimes concurring, but more often dissenting—can encourage continued opposition to the ruling. That is the reason Chief Justice Earl Warren worked so hard to get a unanimous ruling in the school desegregation case. And that is one reason why opponents to abortion continue to push for a ban on the procedure. In *Roe* v. *Wade*, the 1973 case that established the right of a woman to choose abortion, seven of the justices joined the majority position. However, in subsequent rulings, the vote has been much closer—often 5 to 4—in upholding the abortion right.

Because the Court relies so heavily on precedent, separate opinions play a key role when lawyers attempt to change the law. In *Brown* v. *Board of Education*, the lawyers arguing for school desegregation quoted Justice John Marshall Harlan's stinging dissent in *Plessy* v. *Ferguson*, the 1896 case that cemented segregation in place for more than half a century. Harlan had proclaimed the constitution "color-blind," and insisted that "the arbitrary separation of citizens on the basis of race . . . cannot be justified upon any legal grounds." Even though his views did not influence the Court at the time to reverse its stand, Harlan's prestige and eloquence helped persuade a more liberal Court years later.

JUSTICE HUGO L. BLACK VOTED WITH THE MAJORITY IN THE *GAULT* CASE, BUT HE BELIEVED THAT THE ARIZONA LAW UNDER WHICH GERALD WAS SENTENCED VIOLATED THE FIFTH AND SIXTH AMENDMENTS.

argued that the Court had no such power, and that the Arizona statute should be overturned because it violated the Fifth and Sixth Amendments, not because justices thought it was unfair.

> Freedom in this Nation will be far less secure the very moment that it is decided that judges can

determine which of these safeguards "should" or "should not be imposed" according to their notions of what constitutional provisions are consistent with the "traditions and conscience of our people."

In his separate opinion, Justice Harlan concurred in part and dissented in part with the majority. The Court, he said, should impose on the juvenile court only those requirements needed to make the proceedings fair. Using that guideline, Harlan wrote that juvenile courts should be required to do three things:

· notify juveniles and their parents of the charges against young suspects;
· notify juveniles and their parents of their right to hire a lawyer if they choose; and
· keep a written record so the proceedings can be reviewed.

In cases where juveniles faced confinement in an institution, poor youngsters should be told that the state may appoint lawyers for them, Harlan noted. The three requirements would give young suspects "the tools with which their rights could be fully vindicated," while allowing states to follow the procedures they believed necessary to accomplish their goals "without unnecessary hindrance." Harlan opposed extending the rights to remain silent and to confront and cross-examine witnesses to juveniles because such a move "might radically alter the character of juvenile court proceedings."

He contended the states should be given the chance to develop alternatives to make sure juveniles were treated fairly. Harlan said he feared the "rigid procedural requirements" imposed by the Court would hamper "enlightened

JUSTICE BYRON R. WHITE WAS SWORN IN AS A MEMBER OF THE U.S. SUPREME COURT IN 1962. HE VOTED WITH THE MAJORITY IN THE *IN RE* GAULT CASE, BUT HE QUESTIONED WHETHER JUVENILES SHOULD BE GRANTED THE RIGHT TO REMAIN SILENT.

development of the systems of juvenile courts" and discourage efforts to find creative solutions to juvenile crime. Despite his misgivings, he nevertheless voted with the majority because he believed that the court did not provide the Gaults with adequate notice of the charges against Gerald, that they were not informed of their right to counsel, and that the court failed to keep a record of the proceedings. "Gerald Gault," Harlan concluded, "was deprived of his liberty without due process of law."

Justice Byron White concurred with Fortas's opinion except for the reference to self-incrimination. There was no evidence, the justice wrote, that Gerald had been forced to confess, and it was unclear whether the court had advised him of his right to remain silent. White cautioned the Court to "proceed with some care in extending the privilege [against self-incrimination] . . . to proceedings in juvenile court, particularly the nonadjudicatory stages of those proceedings." White also believed that the Court should not have used the Gault case to make a ruling on cross-examination of witnesses in juvenile court. But White supported the Court's decision to rule in Gerald's favor on the other grounds cited in Fortas's opinion.

DISSENT

Justice Potter Stewart, the only dissenter in the Gault case, called the decision "wholly unsound as a matter of constitutional law, and sadly unwise as a matter of judicial policy." He noted that juvenile proceedings were not criminal trials and should not be treated as such:

> Whether treating with a delinquent child, a neglected child, a defective child, or a dependent child, a juvenile proceeding's whole purpose and mission is the very opposite of the mission and purpose of a prosecution in a criminal court. The object of the one is correction of a condition. The object of the other is conviction and punishment for a criminal act.

The *In re Gault* decision, Stewart maintained, served to "convert a juvenile proceeding into a criminal prosecution." He acknowledged that juvenile courts in many areas had "fallen disappointingly short" of the original goals and that much remained to be done to improve the system. But imposing "the Court's long catalog of requirements" on the juvenile court system, Stewart said, invited a "long step backwards into the nineteenth century." Back then, the justice noted, children were tried as adults and received harsh sentences, sometimes even death. He cited the case of a twelve-year-old boy who was hanged after being found guilty of murder. "It was all very constitutional," he noted.

While states must adhere to due process, Stewart said, they should not have to follow "all the technical niceties of a criminal indictment" in juvenile proceedings. Children's cases needed more flexibility and informality, he said. Furthermore, the Gaults knew of their rights and were aware of the charges against Gerald, according to Stewart. The Court, he concluded, should have dismissed Gerald's appeal.

seven
AFTERMATH

HAILED AS A LANDMARK DECISION by the press, the *In re Gault* ruling immediately won support from an impressive list of legal experts, child welfare proponents, juvenile judges, and national organizations. A spokesman for the American Civil Liberties Union, which had financed the Gaults' Supreme Court battle, said the ruling "may be the most important in the present term." Monrad Paulsen, professor of law at Columbia Law School, supported the decision, saying it was long overdue. "What this case means in its most dramatic terms is that, for 68 years we've been putting youngsters into juvenile institutions by procedures which we now learn have been unconstitutional," he said. An expert on juvenile justice, Paulsen predicted few would find fault with the Court's ruling in the case. The National Council on Crime and Delinquency, the National Council of Juvenile Court Judges, and the American Parents Committee also cheered the decision.

Even one of the judges who had helped write the *amicus* brief opposing Gerald Gault's petition conceded that he supported most of the provisions in Fortas's opinion. Don J. Young, a federal judge who wrote much of the brief for Ohio Association of Juvenile Court Judges, said he agreed that juveniles should have a right to counsel and to cross-examine witnesses, and to be warned of their right against self-incrimination. Calling the controversy "a tempest in a teapot," Young said he doubted that the new safeguards would have "any tremendous practical impact" on juvenile courts. But he expressed concern that the ruling might turn juvenile proceedings into mini versions of adult court. "Children aren't supposed to be treated as adults," he told a *New York Times* reporter.

major changes required

Despite Young's prediction, the *In re Gault* opinion led to major changes in the nation's juvenile court system. In Congress, Representative Roman C. Pucinski, D-Illinois, proposed allocating $100 million toward improving the juvenile courts' rehabilitation and treatment programs. "The [Gault] decision means that many hard-core delinquents . . . will be walking the streets unless there are adequate facilities to care for them," he said. Pucinski noted that many parents, working with the courts to help their children, would "see to it that the youngsters waive their procedural safeguards"—but only if there were effective programs in place. "Under present circumstances," the legislator said, "there is no reason to waive [the child's rights]." Congress incorporated the proposal into the Juvenile Delinquency Prevention Act of 1968, which allocated $150 million over three years to states and local governments for services for delinquent youths.

Norman Dorsen, who argued Gerald Gault's case before the Supreme Court, said the decision "significantly altered" the juvenile justice system. "It made the system fairer because more juveniles have lawyers," he said. But the decision, he noted, did not cure juvenile delinquency or stop juvenile crime. And major changes in society altered the system even more.

As time went on, it became clear that living up to the *Gault* requirements would pose serious problems for states and their juvenile courts. When the Court issued its ruling in 1967, only New York, California, Minnesota, and the District of Columbia provided free attorneys for juveniles. In some cases attorneys were provided only when the charge would have been a felony in adult court. The *In re Gault* decision forced states to provide lawyers for thousands of poor young suspects. Frank Lewis told of the reaction of one governor to the *In re Gault* decision. During a 1970 convention of the Association of Trial Lawyers of America, Lewis's mother served on a panel focusing on the problems of cities and states. New Jersey Governor Richard Hughes stood up during the question-and-answer period and pointed at Amelia Lewis. "That lady," he told the gathering, "cost me $150 million last year."

Despite the Supreme Court ruling in *Gault*, states have not always complied, especially concerning the right to counsel. In a 1973 study, the Children's Defense Fund found that in one state one county always granted its juvenile offenders the rights listed in the *Gault* decision, while another county in the same state never provided such rights. In studies conducted by sociologist Barry C. Feld in 1984 and 1989, youthful offenders in some cities were represented by lawyers 90 percent of the time. In a few rural areas, however, fewer than 10 percent of the youth before juvenile court had lawyers. In 1988, California provided counsel to juveniles in at least 85 percent of the cases. New York juveniles had attorneys 96 percent of the time, and Pennsylvania juveniles had attorneys in 86 percent of the cases. But juveniles in more rural areas did not fare as well. A 1990 study in Missouri showed that 39.6 percent of juvenile offenders in urban areas had lawyers, while only 5.3 percent of rural youth were represented by counsel.

In 2005, all states had laws recognizing juveniles' right to counsel. However, in some states, youths did not have lawyers to represent them because they either did not qualify for counsel appointed by the state or they (or their parents) waived the right. In his research Feld suggests that in some cases parents may not want to pay for lawyers for their children and may waive their right to an attorney. In other cases, he says, judges may encourage parents not to bother with the hassle of hiring a lawyer. In 1979, the Supreme Court ruled in *Fare* v. *Michael C.* that juveniles could waive their right to an attorney as long as it could be shown they knew what they were doing. However, many child experts question whether children, especially those under fifteen, have the ability to make such a decision without help from a professional.

Later court cases

Court rulings following *In re Gault* have offered a mixed bag of rights and limitations to juveniles. In a 1970 case, *In re Winship*, the U.S. Supreme Court ruled that states must prove juveniles' guilt beyond a reasonable doubt in all delinquency hearings. The same standard is used in adult criminal trials.

While *In re Gault* addressed juvenile rights during trial and sentencing, lower federal courts extended protections to youths after they had been sentenced. For example, a federal court in Texas used a 1973 case, *Morales* v. *Turman*, to outlaw cruel and unusual punishment of children in state reform schools and other institutions. The ruling specifically banned beatings, druggings, and excessive solitary confinement.

In 1975 the U.S. Supreme Court extended to juveniles the Fifth Amendment right guaranteeing that defendants cannot be prosecuted or punished twice for the same offense. Before the ruling, in *Breed* v. *Jones*, some juveniles were tried in both juvenile and adult courts for the same misdeeds.

The Court, in *Moran* v. *Burbine*, a 1986 case, ruled that a juvenile did not have to request an attorney, that the states should provide a lawyer automatically unless the young offender waived the right to an attorney.

Other rulings have limited the rights of juveniles. In a 1971 case, *McKeiver* v. *Pennsylvania*, the Court ruled that juveniles were not entitled to a trial by jury. Written by Justice Harry A. Blackmun, the majority opinion noted that juveniles benefited from keeping their cases private and that a jury trial would make juvenile proceedings more formal, less flexible, and public:

> There is a possibility, at least, that the jury trial, if required as a matter of constitutional precept, will remake the juvenile proceeding into a fully adversary process and will put an effective end to what has been the idealistic prospect of an intimate, informal protective proceeding.

The Court's ruling in *Schall* v. *Martin* in 1984 upheld the right of juvenile courts to detain juveniles while their cases are processed.

In 1988, the Court upheld the view that children should be treated differently from adults. The ruling in *Thompson* v. *Oklahoma* stated that juveniles were entitled to less harsh sentences than adults because of their immaturity.

> Inexperience, less education, and less intelligence make the teenager less able to evaluate the consequences of his or her conduct while at the same time he or she is much more apt to be motivated by mere emotion or peer pressure than is an adult. The reasons why juveniles are not trusted

IN A 1971 DECISION, JUSTICE HARRY A. BLACKMUN WROTE THAT JUVENILES BENEFITED FROM KEEPING THEIR CASES PRIVATE.

with the privileges and responsibilities of an adult also explain why their irresponsible conduct is not as morally reprehensible as that of an adult.

Though the Court ruled in *Thompson* that a fifteen-year-old was too young to be sentenced to death, a later case, *Stanford* v. *Kentucky*, upheld the death penalty for sixteen- and seventeen-year-olds. In the 5 to 4 decision, issued in 1989, the Court noted that twenty-five states allowed the death penalty for seventeen-year-olds, and twenty-two of those states allowed sixteen-year-olds to be put to death. Therefore, the Court reasoned, there was no national consensus that sentencing teens older than fifteen to death was cruel and unusual. The Court later overturned that ruling in another closely decided case, *Roper* v.

116

Simmons, in 2005. Again, by a vote of 5 to 4, the Court held that the Eighth and Fourteenth Amendments barred the death penalty for defendants who committed their crimes before the age of eighteen. The Eighth Amendment prohibits "cruel and unusual punishments." Justice Anthony Kennedy wrote in his majority opinion:

> When a juvenile offender commits a heinous crime, the State can exact forfeiture of some of the most basic liberties, but the State cannot extinguish his life and his potential to attain a mature understanding of his own humanity.

The Court's decision in *Stanford* no longer applied, according to Kennedy, because the national consensus had changed. Since the *Stanford* decision, thirty states barred executing juveniles and only six states had put teens under eighteen to death. Only three states had executed juveniles in the ten years before the *Roper* case. Kennedy also noted that juveniles lack the maturity of adults, are more vulnerable to outside influences, and have characters that are not as well-formed as those of adults. The Court's ruling reconfirmed what proponents of the juvenile justice system had contended for years: that youths are different from adults and therefore should be treated under a separate justice system.

ADULT V. JUVENILE COURT

For almost three decades following the *In re Gault* decision, crime rates among youth rose alarmingly and publicity focused attention on violent crimes committed by juveniles. The President's Commission on Crime reported in 1967 that "enormous numbers of young people appear to be involved" in criminal acts and juvenile delinquency. According to the report, 223 of every 100,000 youths age fifteen to seventeen were arrested for violent crimes in 1965. That number steadily increased to about 500 in every 100,000 in 1994. An angry and increasingly fearful public pressured lawmakers to pass legislation to protect them from youthful offenders. Instead of providing treatment for troubled youths, the new laws centered on punishment and penalties for juveniles. Many states passed laws that allowed youngsters—some as young as ten—to be tried in adult courts. Officials also instituted other changes including mandatory sentences.

Crime rates for both juveniles and adults have been declining in the United States since 1994. According to data from the Uniform Crime Reports collected by the Federal Bureau of Investigation, the rate for arrests of juveniles for serious crimes fell 48 percent between 1994 and 2003. Preliminary data show that crime rates continue to drop each year. Even so, because of population growth the number of youths involved in the criminal justice system has exploded since the 1960s when Gerald Gault's case was heard. In 1965, the year the Arizona Supreme Court denied Gerald's appeal, the nation's juvenile courts handled 601,000 young offenders. In 2003, U.S. police arrested 2.2 million people under age eighteen.

Despite state laws requiring that certain juvenile cases be sent to adult criminal courts, most youths arrested for crimes continue to be sent to juvenile courts. In fact, the proportion of juvenile cases sent to juvenile courts has been steadily growing. According to the Office of Juvenile Justice and Delinquency Prevention, 58 percent of the cases of arrested youths went to juvenile courts in 1980; that percentage had increased to 71 percent in 2003.

Still, slightly more than a quarter of a million cases involving youths under the age of eighteen are handled in adult courts each year, reveals a study issued in 2005 by the National Coalition for Juvenile Justice. Juvenile judges transfer a small fraction of the cases to adult court. More cases involving juveniles are filed directly in adult courts by prosecutors. The vast majority of the cases, however, are automatically sent to adult court because of state laws that require such action. Some states have set adulthood at age sixteen or seventeen, thus forcing older teens accused of wrongdoing into adult court. Other youngsters end up in adult court because they are accused of a crime that state law has removed from the juvenile court jurisdiction. Thirty-four states have laws that bar juveniles who have gone to trial in adult court on one charge from ever appearing in juvenile court again. All future charges against them, whether for misdemeanors or felonies, must be heard in adult court. Even with the crime rate dropping, many people continue to press for more transfers to adult courts, which they believe offer harsher treatment of juvenile offenders.

Critics and proponents of juvenile courts both point to the problems that plague the system. Public defenders and attorneys appointed to represent poor juveniles are inundated with work. Those who represent youths, as well as prosecutors and judges, often lack experience and see juvenile courts only as training grounds for other posts. In many jurisdictions, juvenile courts and programs do not receive the funding required to fill the needs of troubled youths. The handling of juvenile cases varies widely depending on the jurisdiction and the juvenile's history; this can result in unfair treatment. With the vast number of cases to be considered, many juvenile courts cannot devote the time and resources necessary for individual treatment. And finally, many of the facilities where youths are held do not meet health and safety standards and offer little treatment.

Legal expert Barry Feld and others believe the juvenile court system is not working and should be abolished. Feld, a University of Minnesota law professor and leading expert in juvenile justice, says all crimes should be handled in adult court. He contends that the U.S. Supreme Court ruling in *In re Gault* and other cases forced juvenile courts to become an adversarial system. Since then, according to these experts, the juvenile courts have focused on crimes rather than the individual needs of children. They note that a number of states already allow children to be tried in adult criminal court. In their view, not only has the juvenile justice system failed to rehabilitate youthful offenders; it also deprives them of full constitutional rights.

Under Feld's proposed system, youngsters would have the same rights as adults in court, including a trial by jury. Young defendants, however, would receive shorter sentences based on their age. For example, sentences for seventeen-year-olds would be reduced by one-quarter those given adults convicted of the same offense; sixteen-year-olds would receive sentences half as long as those for adults.

But other legal experts hold out hope that the juvenile justice system can be saved. They believe adult court is not the place to deal with juveniles. Even with its flaws, they see juvenile courts as offering a better way to serve both juveniles and society as a whole. According to the Coalition for Juvenile Justice study, shipping juveniles to adult court does not provide better protection against young offenders, despite what the public may think. Some juveniles transferred to adult court (about one-fifth) actually get less severe penalties than they would have in juvenile court. The coalition study also reported that juveniles sentenced in adult courts are more likely to commit new crimes.

Proponents note that the safeguards required by the Supreme Court affected only juvenile court proceedings to determine a youth's guilt or innocence. The court continues to deal with the individual needs of youths when deciding

Walter Stawarz IV, sixteen, walks from the Beaver County Court in Pennsylvania after being charged as an adult in the beating of a younger boy.

sentencing or treatment. Adult courts, they point out, sentence defendants based on the crime and cannot provide treatment based on an individual youth's circumstances.

Still others argue for a modified system that addresses youths' problems while protecting the public from violent criminals. Juvenile courts, they say, may not be the answer for some youthful offenders—those who continually break the law and those who commit the most serious crimes. But, they say, juvenile courts benefit both troubled youths and society by focusing not only on rights but on rehabilitation for young offenders.

"Unlike criminal court, juvenile court places its emphasis on the best interests of the offender and on the disposition or problem resolution stage instead of on the process of finding guilt," say the authors of a 2005

state laws on juveniles

Each of the nation's fifty states has its own unique juvenile justice system. While U.S. Supreme Court rulings requiring due process for juveniles apply to every state, there is no universal system of dealing with troubled youth. Once a state line is crossed, a juvenile offender is bound by a whole new set of rules and regulations. Depending on where a crime is committed, a person under eighteen may or may not be considered a juvenile, may or may not have the case reviewed by juvenile court, and may or may not be subject to a public hearing.

Some state laws allow prosecutors the option of filing certain charges against youths in juvenile or adult court. Other states require that juvenile cases involving certain crimes be filed in adult court. These laws may also include a minimum age or past criminal activity in order for the defendant to be tried as an adult. Some jurisdictions allow juvenile court judges to determine where any case should be heard. In other states, judges can decide to transfer cases to adult courts only in violent crimes like murder. More than twenty states set no minimum age limit for transferring cases of juveniles charged with certain crimes. Only when the decision to transfer is made by a judge is the youth entitled to a hearing on where his or her case should be heard.

The tables below illustrate the hodgepodge of laws and procedures that govern juvenile offenses across the nation:

age of adulthood states
Age 16 Connecticut, New York, North Carolina
Age 17 Georgia, Illinois, Louisiana, Massachusetts, Michigan, Missouri, New Hampshire, South Carolina, Texas, Wisconsin
Age 18 All other states

STATES THAT ALLOW PROSECUTORS TO FILE CHARGES DIRECTLY IN ADULT COURT

Arizona, Arkansas, California, Colorado, District of Columbia, Florida, Georgia, Louisiana, Michigan, Montana, Nebraska, Oklahoma, Vermont, Virginia, Wyoming

STATES WITH ONCE-AN-ADULT-ALWAYS-AN-ADULT LAWS

Alabama, Arizona, California, Delaware, District of Columbia. Florida, Hawaii, Idaho, Illinois, Indiana, Iowa, Kansas, Maine, Maryland, Michigan, Minnesota, Mississippi, Missouri, Nevada, New Hampshire, North Carolina, North Dakota, Ohio, Oklahoma, Oregon, Pennsylvania, Rhode Island, South Dakota, Tennessee, Texas, Utah, Virginia, Washington, Wisconsin

STATES THAT PROVIDE PUBLIC HEARINGS

*Alaska, *Arizona, *California, *Colorado, *Delaware, *Florida, *Georgia, Hawaii, Idaho, Illinois, *Indiana, *Iowa, Kansas, *Louisiana, *Maine, *Maryland, *Massachusetts, *Michigan, Minnesota, *Missouri, *Montana, *Nevada, *New Jersey, *New Mexico, *New York, Ohio, *Oklahoma, Pennsylvania, South Dakota, Texas, Utah, Virginia, *Washington, *Wisconsin

* no age limit for certain crimes

study on the juvenile justice system. "Juvenile court is dedicated specifically to not ruining the life chances of offenders by imposing exceptionally harsh dispositions and permanent, debilitating records. . . . Rather than sending all juvenile offenders to criminal court and abolishing juvenile court, the more balanced and logical answer seems to be to preserve juvenile court for the vast majority of, but certainly not all, juvenile offenders."

GAULT STILL A LANDMARK

Despite the problems that continue to plague the juvenile justice system, *In re Gault* stands as a landmark case that helped protect the children who found themselves at the mercy of the court. In the Gault case, the Supreme Court, for the first time, opened the doors of the juvenile courts and gave children some of the rights in the Constitution. Robert F. Drinan, law professor at Georgetown University who also served as a member of Congress, described the impact of *In re Gault* this way:

> *Gault* did not give [the child] the entire panoply of due process, but the thrust is in that direction. We cannot mistreat him, we cannot say that he is a non-citizen. . . . *Gault* means in the long run that no child, simply because he is a child, may be deprived of a basic right without some type of due process.

Looking back on the case that changed his life four decades ago, Gerald Gault is still stung by the injustice done to him. "When you're taken away from your family without so much as a phone call and they don't even know where you are, that's not right," he said. But he remembers, too, the fighting spirit of his parents and the rights they won for the nation's youth. "It was a hard time for them," he said, "but they fought for what was right."

notes

Introduction

p. 10, par. 3, Keith Snyder, "An Interview with Anthony A.
'Tony' Guarna, Montgomery County Chief JPO,"
Pennsylvania Juvenile Justice, 8, no. 2 (February 2000), 1–3.

p. 11, par. 2, Coalition for Juvenile Justice. *Childhood on Trial:
The Failure of Trying and Sentencing Youth in Adult Criminal
Court*. Washington, DC: Coalition for Juvenile Justice,
March 2005, 6.

Chapter 1

p. 13, par. 2, "U.S. Supreme Court cases have had an impact on
the character and procedures of the juvenile justice
system," *Bulletin: Juvenile Justice: A Century of Change*.
Washington, DC: National Report Series, Juvenile Justice,
December 1999.
http://www.ncjrs.gov/html/ojjdp/9912_2/juv2.html

p. 14, par. 2, Gerald Gault, interview with author, March 8,
1995.

p. 14, par. 3, Appellants' brief, *U.S. Reports*, *In re Gault* case
file, No. 116, 34.

p. 15, par. 3, Appellants' brief, *U.S. Reports*, *In re Gault* case
file, No. 116, 33.

p. 15, par. 4, *In re Gault*, 387 U.S. 1 (1967), 6.

p. 16, par. 1, *In re Gault*, 7, 9.

p. 16, par. 5, *In re Gault*, footnote 6.

p. 17, par. 1, *In re Gault*, 9.

p. 17, par. 3, Robert E. Shepherd Jr., "Still Seeking the Promise of Gault: Juveniles and the Right to Counsel," *Criminal Justice Magazine*, 18, no. 2 (summer 2003), 22–27.

p. 17, par. 4, Appellants' brief, *U.S. Reports*, *In re Gault* case file, No. 116, 3.

Chapter 2

p. 19, par. 2, Joseph M. Hawes. *The Children's Rights Movement: A History of Advocacy and Protection*. Boston: Twayne Publishers, 1991, 6.

p. 20, par. 2, Sir William Blackstone. *Commentaries 23*. Wendell ed., 1847, quoted in *In re Gault*, 387 U.S. 1 (1967), dissent, 80, footnote 2.

p. 20, par. 3, Leah Eskin, "Punishment or Reform? Juvenile Justice in U.S. History," *Scholastic Update*, 123, no. 14 (April 5, 1991), 18.

p. 21, par. 3, Eskin, "Punishment or Reform?" 18.

p. 22, par. 1, Hawes, *The Children's Rights Movement*, 16.

p. 22, par. 2, Hawes, *The Children's Rights Movement*, 17.

p. 22, par. 3, Hawes, *The Children's Rights Movement*, 17.

p. 23, par. 1, Hawes, *The Children's Rights Movement*, 18.

p. 23, par. 3, "The Orphan Train Movement." New York: Children's Aid Society, 2001–2005. http://www.childrens aidsociety.org/about/train

p. 24, par. 2, Hawes, *The Children's Rights Movement*, 33.

p. 24, par. 3, Eskin, "Punishment or Reform?" 18.

p. 25, par. 3, Eskin, "Punishment or Reform?" 19.

p. 26, par. 1, *In re Gault*, 387 U.S. 1 (1967), 14, footnote 14.

p. 26, par. 2, Jethro K. Lieberman, *Milestones! Two Hundred Years of American Law*. New York: Oxford University Press, 1976, 349.

p. 26, par. 3, *In re Gault*, 22.

p. 28, par. 1, *In re Gault*, footnote 26.

p. 29, par. 3, *Kent v. United States*, 383 U.S. 541, 546–556.

p. 30, par. 1, *Kent v. United States*, 554.

p. 30, par. 3, *Kent v. United States*, 556.

Chapter 3

p. 31, par. 2, Appellants' brief, *U.S. Reports, In re Gault* case file, No. 116, 9.

p. 31, par. 3, Wolfgang Saxon, "Amelia Lewis, 91, Victor in Case That Changed Juvenile Justice." *New York Times* (Nov. 19, 1994), A-31.

p. 34, par. 3, *In re Gault*, 387 U.S. 1 (1967), footnote 5.

p. 35, par. 1, *In re Gault*, 387 U.S. 1 (1967), 5.

p. 36, par. 1, Application of Gault, 99 AZ. 181, 1965–1966 (St. Paul, MN: West Publishing Co., 1966), 188.

p. 36, par. 3, *In re Gault*, 11, footnote 7.

p. 36, par. 4, Application of Gault, 187.

p. 37, par. 2, Wolfgang Saxon, "Amelia Lewis, 91, Victor in Case That Changed Juvenile Justice."

p. 37, par. 3, Gerald Gault, interview with author, March 8, 1995.

Gerald Gault Sidebar, pp. 38–39

Gerald Gault, interview with author, March 8, 1995.

Wolfgang Saxon, "Amelia Lewis, 91, Victor in Case That Changed Juvenile Justice," *New York Times* (November 19, 1994), A-31.

Robert E. Shepherd Jr., "Still Seeking the Promise of Gault: Juveniles and the Right to Counsel," *Criminal Justice Magazine*, 18, no. 2 (summer 2003), 22–27.

Peyton Whitely, "The Boy Who Made Legal History," *Seattle Times* (June 18, 1985), H.3.

p. 41, par. 1, Frank Lewis, interview with author, February 16, 1995.

p. 41, par. 3, Norman Dorsen, interview with author, February 13, 1995.

Chapter 4

p. 49, par. 2, Appellant's brief, *U.S. Reports, In re Gault* case file, No. 116.

Through the Court System Sidebar, pp. 50–52
The Supreme Court Historical Society, http://www.supreme
    courthistory.org
Administrative Office of the U.S. Courts, http://www.
    uscourts.gov
Iowa Court Information System, http://www.judicial.state.
    ia.us/students/6

There is also a diagram on the last Web site.

p. 54, par. 2, The Legal Aid Society and Citizens' Committee for
    New York Inc., *amicus* brief, *In re Gault* case file, No. 116.
p. 55, par. 1, The National Legal Aid and Defender
    Association, *amicus* brief, *In re Gault* case file, No. 116.
p. 55, par. 2, American Parents Committee, *amicus* brief, *In re
    Gault* case file, No. 116.
p. 57, par. 1, *In re Holmes*, 104 Ohio 3d 664 (2004).
p. 57, par. 3, Appellee's brief, *In re Gault* case file, No. 116.
p. 60, par. 3, Appellee's brief, *In re Gault* case file, No. 116.
p. 61, par. 1, Ohio Association of Juvenile Court Judges, *amicus*
    brief, *In re Gault* case file, No. 116.

Chapter 5
p. 63, par. 2, Norman Dorsen, interview with author, February
    13, 1995.
p. 64, par. 3, Dorsen, interview with author, February 13, 1995.
p. 66, par. 3, Dorsen, interview with author, February 13, 1995.
p. 67, par. 2–3, Dorsen, interview with author, February 13, 1995.
p. 67, par. 4, Appellant's oral arguments, *In re Gault*,
    December 5, 1966.

The Fourteenth Amendment Sidebar, pp. 68–71
"Bill of Rights in Action," *Constitutional Rights Foundation*, 7:4
    (Spring 1991), http://www.crf-usa.org/bria/bria7_4.htm#
    second
"The Fourteenth Amendment," Library of Congress,
    http://memory.loc.gov/ammem/today/jul28.html
Permoli v. *Municipality No. 1 of City of New Orleans*, 44 U.S. 589
    (1845).

Slaughterhouse Cases, 83 U.S. 36 (1872).
U.S. Constitution, Amendment XIV.

pp. 72–80, Appellant's oral arguments, *In re Gault*, December 5, 1966.

p. 75, par. 3, *Kent v. United States*, 383 U.S. 541, 555–556.

p. 78, par. 1, Dorsen, interview with author, February 13, 1995.

p. 81, par. 2–p. 89, par. 3, Appellee's oral arguments, *In re Gault*, December 5, 1966.

p. 89, par. 4–p. 92, par. 1, Ohio Association of Juvenile Court Judges *amicus* oral arguments, *In re Gault*, December 5, 1966.

p. 92, par. 2–4, Appellant's oral arguments, *In re Gault*, December 5, 1966.

Chapter 6

p. 96, par. 1–p. 102, par. 2, *In re Gault*, 387 U.S. 1 (1967).

p. 102, par. 3–4, Joseph B. Sanborn Jr. and Anthony W. Salerno. *The Juvenile Justice System: Law and Process*. Los Angeles: Roxbury Publishing Company, 2005, 37.

p. 103, par. 2, Sanborn and Salerno. *The Juvenile Justice System: Law and Process*, 38; Concurrence, Justice Hugo L. Black, *In re Gault*, 387 U.S. 1 (1967).

Justices Speak Their Minds Sidebar, pp. 104–105

Richard Kluger. *Simple Justice*. New York: Alfred A. Knopf, 1976.

Justice John Marshall Harlan, Dissent, *Plessy v. Ferguson*, 163 U.S. 537 (1896).

p. 106, par. 2–p. 107, par. 1, Concurrence, Justice Hugo L. Black, *In re Gault*, 387 U.S. 1 (1967).

p. 107, par. 3–p. 109, par. 1, Concurrence, Justice John Marshall Harlan, *In re Gault*, 387 U.S. 1 (1967).

p. 109, par. 1, Concurrence, Justice Byron White, *In re Gault*, 387 U.S. 1 (1967).

p. 109, par. 3–p. 110, par. 2, Dissent, Justice Potter Stewart, *In re Gault*, 387 U.S. 1 (1967).

Chapter 7

p. 111, par. 1, Sidney E. Zion, "Court Ruling on Juveniles Is Hailed as Ending Unfair Treatment," *New York Times* (May 17, 1967), A-31.

p. 112, par. 1, Zion, *New York Times* (May 17, 1967), A-31.

p. 112, par. 2, Zion, *New York Times* (May 17, 1967), A-31.

p. 112, par. 2, "Juvenile Delinquency Bill Is Sent to the White House," *New York Times* (July 19, 1968), 28.

p. 112, par. 3, Norman Dorsen, interview with author, February 13, 1995.

p. 113, par. 1, Frank Lewis, interview with author, February 16, 1995.

p. 113, par. 2, Happy Craven Fernandez. *The Child Advocacy Handbook.* New York: Pilgrim Press, 1980, 44.

p. 113, par. 2, Barry C. Feld. *Justice for Children: The Right to Counsel and the Juvenile Courts.* Boston: Northeastern University Press, 1993, 54, 28.

p. 114, par. 1, Joseph B. Sanborn Jr. and Anthony W. Salerno. *The Juvenile Justice System: Law and Process.* Los Angeles: Roxbury Publishing Company, 2005, 319–322.

p. 114, par. 1, Feld, *Justice for Children*, 28.

p. 115, par. 4, *McKeiver v. Pennsylvania*, 403 U.S. 528 (1971), 545.

p. 116, par. 1, *Thompson v. Oklahoma*, 487 U.S. 815 (1988), 835.

p. 117, par. 2, *Roper v. Simmons*, 543 U.S. 551 (2005), 20.

p. 118, par. 1, John J. Dilulio Jr., "How Goes the Battle?" *The New Democrat* (July 1, 1999).

p. 118, par. 2, Terry Frieden, "Violent crime rate declines again." *CNN*, October 17, 2005. http://www.cnn.com/2005/LAW/10/17/crime.rate

p. 118, par. 2, "Juvenile Arrests 2003." *Office of Juvenile Justice and Delinquency Prevention Bulletin*, August 2005. http://www.ncjrs.gov/html/ojjdp/209735/intro.html

p. 118, par. 3, "Juvenile Arrests 2003," August 2005, 6. http://www.ncjrs.gov/html/ojjdp/209735/page6.html

p. 118, par. 4, Coalition for Juvenile Justice. "Report Overview," *Childhood on Trial: The Failure of Trying and Sentencing Youth in Adult Criminal Court.* Washington, DC:

Coalition for Juvenile Justice, March 2005, 1.

p. 119, par. 2, Sanborn and Salerno. *The Juvenile Justice System: Law and Process*, 502–505.

p. 120, par. 2, Jeffrey A. Butts, "Can We Do Without Juvenile Justice?" *Criminal Justice Magazine*, 15, no. 1 (spring 2000). https://www.abanet.org/crimjust/cjmag/15-1/butts.html

p. 120, par. 3, "Report Overview," *Childhood on Trial: The Failure of Trying and Sentencing Youth in Adult Criminal Court*, 2.

State Laws on Juveniles Sidebar, pp. 122–123

Joseph B. Sanborn Jr. and Anthony W. Salerno. *The Juvenile Justice System: Law and Process*. Los Angeles: Roxbury Publishing Company, 2005, 519–530.

Coalition for Juvenile Justice. *Childhood on Trial: The Failure of Trying and Sentencing Youth in Adult Criminal Court*. Washington, DC: Coalition for Juvenile Justice, March 2005, 16–20.

Patrick Griffin, "National Overviews," *State Juvenile Justice Profiles*. Pittsburgh, PA: National Center for Juvenile Justice, 2005. http://www.ncjj.org/stateprofiles

p. 124, par. 1, Sanborn and Salerno. *The Juvenile Justice System: Law and Process*, 509.

p. 124, par. 3, Virginia Davis Nordin, ed. *Gault: What Now for the Juvenile Court?* Ann Arbor: Institute of Continuing Legal Education, 1968, 116.

p. 124, par. 5, Gerald Gault, interview with author, March 8, 1995.

All Web sites accessible as of August 7, 2006.

Further Information

BOOKS

Barrett, Paul, Richard Carelli, and Marcia Coyle. *A Year in the Life of the Supreme Court*, Constitutional Conflicts. Durham, NC: Duke University Press, 1995.

Baum, Lawrence. *American Courts: Process and Policy*. Boston: Houghton Mifflin Company, 2001.

Cornelius, Kay. *The Supreme Court, Your Government: How It Works*. Broomall, PA: Chelsea House Publishers, 2000.

Hartman, Gary, Roy M. Mersky, and Cindy L. Tate. *Landmark Supreme Court Cases: The Most Influential Decisions of the Supreme Court*, Facts on File Library of American History. New York: Facts on File, 2004.

Hawes, Joseph M. *The Children's Rights Movement: A History of Advocacy and Protection*. Boston: Twayne Publishers, 1991.

Heath, David, and Charlotte Wilcox. *The Supreme Court of the United States*, American Civics. Mankato, MN: Bridgestone Books, 1999.

Irons, Peter. *The Courage of Their Convictions: Sixteen Americans Who Fought Their Way to the Supreme Court*. New York: Penguin, 1990.

_____. *People's History of the Supreme Court*. New York: Penguin, 2000.

Jacobs, Thomas A. *Teens on Trial: Young People Who Challenged the Law—And Changed Your Life*. Minneapolis: Free Spirit Publishing, 2000.

_____. *What Are My Rights?: 95 Questions and Answers About Teens and the Law*. Minneapolis: Free Spirit Publishing, 1997.

LeVert, Suzanne. *The Supreme Court.* New York: Benchmark
  Books, 2002.
Patrick, John J. *The Supreme Court of the United States: A Student
  Companion*, Oxford Student Companions to American
  Government, 2nd ed. New York: Oxford University Press
  Children's Books, 2002.
Satterthwaite, Marcia. *Juvenile Crime* (Crime, Justice and
  Punishment). Broomall, PA: Chelsea House Publishers,
  1997.
Savage, David G. *The Supreme Court and Individual Rights*, 4th
  ed. Washington, DC: CQ Press, 2004.

VIDEOTAPES/AUDIOTAPES

Irons, Peter, ed. *May It Please the Court: Courts, Kids, and the
  Constitution.* New York: The New York Press, 2000. Live
  recordings and transcripts of the Supreme Court oral argu-
  ments (audio).
*Just The Facts—The United States Bill of Rights and Constitutional
  Amendments*, Just the Facts series. Camarillo, CA: Goldhil
  Home Media I, 2004 (video).
Profiles of Freedom: A Living Bill of Rights. Arlington, VA:
  Bill of Rights Institute, 1997 (video).

WEB SITES

American Bar Association's Juvenile Justice Committee.
  http://www.abanet.org/crimjust/juvjus
American Civil Liberties Union.
  http://www.aclu.org
Coalition for Juvenile Justice.
  http://www.juvjustice.org
Digital History, Steven Mintz, University of Houston.
  http://www.digitalhistory.uh.edu/do_history/young_people
  /voices2.cfm
Federal Bureau of Investigation's Uniform Crime Reports.
  http://www.fbi.gov/ucr/ucr.htm
FindLaw (U.S. Supreme Court Cases).
  http://www.findlaw.com/casecode/supreme.html

"JEC Legal Glossary," Judicial Education Center of New Mexico. http://jec.unm.edu/resources/glossaries/general glossary.htm

Landmark Cases of the U.S. Supreme Court. http://www.landmarkcases.org

'Lectric Law Library. http://www.lectlaw.com/files/case15.htm

Legal Information Institute, Cornell Law School. http://www.law.cornell.edu/supct/html/historics/USSC_CR _0017_0316_ZS.html

National Youth Rights Association. http://www.youthrights.org/inregault.shtml

Office of Juvenile Justice and Delinquency Prevention. http://ojjdp.ncjrs.gov

Oyez Project: U.S. Supreme Court Multimedia Web site. http://www.oyez.org/oyez/frontpage

Supreme Court Historical Society. http://www.supremecourthistory.org

Supreme Court of the United States. http://www.supremecourtus.gov

BIBLIOGraPHY

BOOKS/REPORTS

Coalition for Juvenile Justice. *Childhood on Trial: The Failure of Trying and Sentencing Youth in Adult Criminal Court*. Washington, DC: March 2005.

Feld, Barry C. *Justice for Children: The Right to Counsel and the Juvenile Courts*. Boston: Northeastern University Press, 1993.

Fernandez, Happy Craven. *The Child Advocacy Handbook*. New York: Pilgrim Press, 1980.

Hawes, Joseph M. *The Children's Rights Movement: A History of Advocacy and Protection*. Boston: Twayne Publishers, 1991.

Irons, Peter. *The Courage of Their Convictions: Sixteen Americans Who Fought Their Way to the Supreme Court*. New York: Penguin, 1990.

Irons, Peter, ed. *May It Please the Court: Courts, Kids, and the Constitution*. New York: The New York Press, 2000. Live recordings and transcripts of the Supreme Court oral arguments.

Kluger, Richard. *Simple Justice*. New York: Alfred A. Knopf, 1976.

Lieberman, Jethro K. *Milestones! Two Hundred Years of American Law*. New York: Oxford University Press, 1976.

Nordin, Virginia Davis, ed. *Gault: What Now for the Juvenile Court?* Ann Arbor: Institute of Continuing Legal Education, 1968.

Rudenstine, David. *The Day the Presses Stopped*. Berkeley: University of California Press, 1996.

Sanborn, Joseph B. Jr., and Anthony W. Salerno. *The Juvenile Justice System: Law and Process.* Los Angeles: Roxbury Publishing Company, 2005.

Supreme Court Historical Society. *Supreme Court of the United States* (booklet). Washington, DC: Public Information Office, Supreme Court of the United States, 1979.

Witt, Elder. *Congressional Quarterly's Guide to the U.S. Supreme Court*, 2nd ed. Washington, DC: Congressional Quarterly, 1990.

ARTICLES/INTERVIEWS

Behrman, Richard E., M.D., ed. "The Juvenile Court: Analysis and Recommendations," *The Future of Children*, 6, no. 3 (Winter 1996).

Butts, Jeffrey A. "Can We Do Without Juvenile Justice?" *Criminal Justice Magazine*, 15, no. 1 (Spring 2000). https://www.abanet.org/crimjust/cjmag/15-1/butts.html

Children's Aid Society. "The Orphan Train Movement." New York: Children's Aid Society, 2001–2005. http://www.childrensaidsociety.org/about/train

Eskin, Leah. "Punishment or Reform? Juvenile Justice in U.S. History," *Scholastic Update*, 123, no. 14 (April 5, 1991).

Frieden, Terry. "FBI: Violent crime rate declines again." *CNN*, October 17, 2005. http://www.cnn.com/2005/LAW/10/17/crime.rate

Office of Juvenile Justice and Delinquency Prevention. "Juvenile Arrests 2003." *Office of Juvenile Justice and Delinquency Prevention Bulletin*, August 2005. http://www.ncjrs.gov/html/ojjdp/209735/intro.html

Saxon, Wolfgang. "Amelia Lewis, 91, Victor in Case That Changed Juvenile Justice," *New York Times* (Nov. 19, 1994), A-31.

Shepherd, Robert E. Jr. "Still Seeking the Promise of Gault: Juveniles and the Right to Counsel," *Criminal Justice Magazine*, 18, no. 2 (summer 2003), 22–27.

Snyder, Keith. "An Interview with Anthony A. 'Tony' Guarna, Montgomery County Chief JPO," *Pennsylvania Juvenile Justice*, 8, no. 2, February 2000.

"U.S. Supreme Court cases have had an impact on the character and procedures of the juvenile justice system," *Bulletin: Juvenile Justice: A Century of Change.* Washington, DC: National Report Series, Juvenile Justice, December 1999. http://www.ncjrs.gov/html/ojjdp/9912_2/juv2.html

Whitely, Peyton. "The Boy Who Made Legal History," *Seattle Times* (June 18, 1985), H.3.

Zion, Sidney E. "Court Ruling on Juveniles Is Hailed as Ending Unfair Treatment," *New York Times* (May 17, 1967), A-31.

STATUTES/COURT CASES/DOCUMENTS

Breed v. *Jones*, 421 U.S. 519 (1975).

Escobedo v. *Illinois*, 378 U.S. 478 (1964).

Fare v. *Michael C.*, 442 U.S. 707 (1979).

In re Gault, 387 U.S. 1 (1967).

In re Holmes, 104 Ohio 3d 664 (2004).

In re Winship, 397 U.S. 358 (1970).

Kent v. *United States*, 383 U.S. 541 (1966).

McKeiver v. *Pennsylvania*, 403 U.S. 528 (1971).

Miranda v. *Arizona*, 384 U.S. 436 (1966).

Morales v. *Turman*, 430 U.S. 322 (1977).

Moran v. *Burbine*, 475 U.S. 412 (1986).

New York Times v. *United States*, 403 U.S. 713 (1971).

Plessy v. *Ferguson*, 163 U.S. 537 (1896).

Roper v. *Simmons*, 543 U.S. 551 (2005).

Schall v. *Martin*, 467 U.S. 253 (1984).

Stanford v. *Noucky*, 492 U.S. 361 (1989).

Thompson v. *Oklahoma*, 487 U.S. 815 (1988).

U.S. Constitution.

WEB SITES

Administrative Office of the U.S. Courts.
    http://www.uscourts.gov

American Bar Association's Juvenile Justice Committee.
    http://www.abanet.org/crimjust/juvjus

American Civil Liberties Union.
    http://www.aclu.org

Coalition for Juvenile Justice.
  http://www.juvjustice.org
Federal Bureau of Investigation's Uniform Crime Reports.
  http://www.fbi.gov/ucr/ucr.htm
FindLaw (U.S. Supreme Court Cases).
  http://www.findlaw.com/casecode/supreme.html
Iowa Court Information System.
  http://www.judicial.state.ia.us/students/6
JEC Legal Glossary, Judicial Education Center of New Mexico.
  http://jec.unm.edu/resources/glossaries/general-
  glossary.htm
Landmark Cases of the U.S. Supreme Court.
  http://www.landmarkcases.org
Legal Information Institute, Cornell Law School.
  http://www.law.cornell.edu
National Archives and Records Administration, "Civil War and
  Reconstruction (1850–1877)."
  http://www.archives.gov/exhibits/american_originals/
  scott.html
National Youth Rights Association.
  http://www.youthrights.org/inregault.shtml
Office of Juvenile Justice and Delinquency Prevention.
  http://ojjdp.ncjrs.gov
Oyez Project: U.S. Supreme Court Multimedia Web Site.
  http://www.oyez.org/oyez/frontpage
Supreme Court Historical Society.
  http://www.supremecourthistory.org
Supreme Court of the United States.
  http://www.supremecourtus.gov

All Web sites accessible as of August 7, 2006.

index

Page numbers in **boldface** are illustrations, tables, and charts.

about the author

susan DUDLEY GOLD has worked as a reporter for a daily newspaper, managing editor of two statewide business magazines, and freelance writer for several regional publications. She has written more than three dozen books for middle-school and high-school students on a variety of topics, including American history, health issues, law, and space.

Gold's *The Panama Canal Transfer: Controversy at the Crossroads* won first place in the nonfiction juvenile book category in the National Federation of Press Women's communications contest. Her book, *Sickle Cell Disease*, was named Best Book (science) by the Society of School Librarians International, as well as earning placement on *Appraisal*'s top ten "Best Books" list. The American Association for the Advancement of Science honored another of her books, *Asthma*, as one of its "Best Books for Children." She has written several titles in the Supreme Court Milestones series for Marshall Cavendish.

In 2001 Gold received a Jefferson Award for community service in recognition of her work with a support group for people with chronic pain, which she founded in 1993. She and her husband, John Gold, own and operate a Web design and publishing business in Maine. They have one son, Samuel.